Artificial Neural Networks and Neural Processing

Artificial Neural Networks and Neural Processing

Partha Ghosh

Department of Computer Science and Engineering, Govt. College of Engineering and Ceramic Technology, Kolkata, India

and

Suradhuni Ghosh

Department of Geography, Govt. Girls' General Degree College, Kolkata, India

CWP

This edition has been published by Central West Publishing PTY LTD, (ABN 13 683 898 722) Australia
© 2026 Central West Publishing PTY LTD

For more information about the books published by Central West Publishing PTY LTD, please visit https://centralwestpublishing.com

Disclaimer
Every effort has been made by the publisher, editors and authors while preparing this book, however, no warranties are made regarding the accuracy and completeness of the content. The publisher, editors and authors disclaim without any limitation all warranties as well as any implied warranties about sales, along with fitness of the content for a particular purpose. Citation of any website and other information sources does not mean any endorsement from the publisher, editors and authors. For ascertaining the suitability of the contents contained herein for a particular lab or commercial use, consultation with the subject expert is needed. In addition, while using the information and methods contained herein, the practitioners and researchers need to be mindful for their own safety, along with the safety of others, including the professional parties and premises for whom they have professional responsibility. To the fullest extent of law, the publisher, editors and authors are not liable in all circumstances (special, incidental, and consequential) for any injury and/or damage to persons and property, along with any potential loss of profit and other commercial damages due to the use of any methods, products, guidelines, procedures contained in the material herein.

NATIONAL LIBRARY OF AUSTRALIA

A catalogue record for this book is available from the National Library of Australia

ISBN (print): 978-1-922617-73-6

Preface

Artificial intelligence has advanced thanks to advances in machine learning. Deep learning is often regarded as the most sophisticated method for solving complicated issues involving enormous data sets. We shall study what a neural network is and how it can manage difficult data-driven challenges in this section.

The main purpose of a neural network is to simulate the operation of a human brain and was modelled after the human brain. The human brain is a neural network composed of many neurons, while an artificial neural network (ANN) is composed of a substantial number perceptrons. In artificial neural networks (ANNs), the output of a node or neuron is determined by the activation function of that node or neuron for a certain input or combination of inputs. The divide between people and robots has been bridged by AI, which has advanced significantly. The goal of the area of computer vision is to equip and programme machines to see the environment the same way that people do. Computer vision employs this understanding for tasks like image recognition, analysis, and classification. Particularly with the convolutional neural network technique, deep learning has proved successful in computer vision.

Introduction

Artificial Intelligence has advanced thanks to advances in Machine Learning. Deep Learning is often regarded as the most sophisticated method for solving complicated issues involving enormous data sets. We shall study what a Neural Network is and how it can manage difficult data-driven challenges in this section.

The main purpose of a Neural Network is to simulate the operation of a human brain and was modelled after the human brain. The human brain is a neural network composed of many neurons, while an Artificial Neural Network (ANN) is composed of a substantial number perceptrons (described below).

In artificial neural networks (ANNs), the output of a node or neuron is determined by the activation function of that node or neuron for a certain input or combination of inputs. The divide between people and robots has been bridged by AI, which has advanced significantly. The goal of the area of computer vision is to equip and programme machines to see the environment the same way that people do. Computer vision employs this understanding for tasks like image recognition, analysis, and classification. Particularly with the Convolutional Neural Network technique, Deep Learning has proved successful in computer vision.

What is Machine Learning?

A subfield of AI and computer science called "machine learning" aims to replicate human learning processes via the use of data and algorithms. Self-driving vehicles and Netflix's recommendation engine are just two examples of the unique goods it has made possible. The rapidly expanding discipline of data science includes machine learning as a crucial component. Data science use statistical techniques to classify data, forecast outcomes, and unearth valuable insights. The market will require more data scientists as big data continues to develop and thrive [1].

What is Deep Learning?

Deep learning, a branch of machine learning, is focused on self-improvement through analysis of computer algorithms. It operates using artificial neural networks created to mimic how people think and learn. Larger, more complicated neural networks are now possible thanks to developments in big data analytics. This makes it possible for computers to watch, understand, and respond to complex events more quickly than people. Deep learning has benefited in the categorization of images, language translation, and speech recognition, and it may be used to automatically resolve any pattern recognition issue [2].

Example of Deep Learning at Work

A neural network's objective is to identify images that have dogs in them. To do this, a training set of images that contains several illustrations of dog faces and photographs of items that aren't dogs must be gathered. As the photos are input into the neural network, various nodes assign weights to various components. The final output layer combines the information that at first glance appears to be unrelated, such as hairy, has a nose, and has four legs, and produces the result: dog.

If there is a match between the neural network's response and a human-generated label, the output is validated. If not, the neural network detects the mistake and modifies its weightings. Even when the neural networks are not explicitly instructed what constitutes a dog, this training method, known as supervised learning, nevertheless takes place. They must gradually identify patterns in the data and acquire new skills on their own.

Applications of Deep Learning

Deep learning is used to recognise people and things in photos, comprehend speech, predict the weather, and assist advertisers in real-time bidding and targeted display advertising. It can anticipate the weather, comprehend speech, identify people and objects in pictures, and assist marketers in using data for real-time bidding and targeted display advertising.

Importance of Deep Learning

Deep learning can handle both organised and unstructured data, in contrast to machine learning, which can only handle the former. While machine learning algorithms struggle to handle complicated operations well, deep learning algorithms can. Machine learning techniques employ tagged sample data to uncover patterns, whereas deep learning processes massive amounts of data as input to extract features. Deep learning is required to keep the model operating at its peak performance [3].

The Idea of Neural Network – Perceptron

Frank Rosenblatt first created perceptrons in 1957, making them one of the earliest computer models of neural networks. They serve as the building blocks for deeper, more complicated networks and are a simplified representation of a biological neuron.

So how do perceptrons work? A perceptron takes several binary inputs, $x1, x2, ...,$ and produces a single binary output as in **Figure 1**:

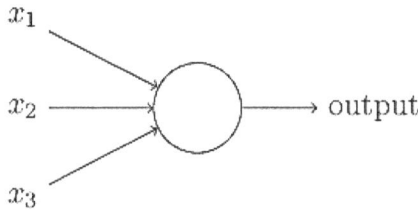

Figure 1: A perceptron generates a single binary output from many binary inputs.

In the example shown the perceptron has three inputs $x1, x2, x3$. To determine a multi-input system's output, Rosenblatt suggested a rule. He introduced *weights*, $w1, w2, ...,$ real numbers expressing the importance of the respective inputs to the output. The neuron's

3

output, 0 *or* 1 is determined by whether the weighted sum $\sum_j w_j x_j$ is less than or greater than some *threshold value.*
A parameter of the neuron, comparable to weights, the threshold is a real value:

$$output = \begin{cases} 0 \ if \ \sum_j w_j x_j \leq threshold \\ 1 \ if \ \sum_j w_j x_j > threshold \end{cases}$$

Let's simplify the way we describe perceptrons. The condition $\sum_j w_j x_j > threshold$ is cumbersome, and we can make two notational changes to simplify it. The first change is to write $\sum_j w_j x_j$ as a dot product,$w \cdot x \equiv \sum_j w_j x_j$ where w and x are vectors whose components are the weights and inputs, respectively. The second change is to move the threshold to the other side of the inequality, and to replace it by what's known as the perceptron's *bias, $b \equiv -threshold$*. Using the bias instead of the threshold, the perceptron rule can be rewritten:

$$output = \begin{cases} 0 \ if \ w \cdot x + b \leq 0 \\ 1 \ if \ w \cdot x + b > 0 \end{cases}$$

The bias represents the ease with which a perceptron can fire or output a 1. It serves as a gauge of how simple it is to trigger the perceptron [4].

Implements of a NAND Gate:

Perceptrons are used to calculate basic logical operations like AND, OR, and NAND as well as to analyse evidence and make judgements. For instance, the perceptron in **Figure 2** has two inputs, each with a weight of -2, and an overall bias of 3. Here's our perceptron:

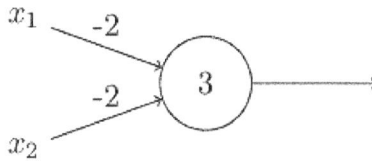

Figure 2: A perceptron with two inputs each with weight -2, and an overall bias of 3.

Then we see that input 00 produces output 1, since $(-2) * 0 + (-2) * 0 + 3 = 3$ is positive. The * symbol is used to make multiplications explicit, showing that inputs 01 and 10 produce output 1. But the input 11 produces output 0, since $(-2) * 1 + (-2) * 1 + 3 = -1$ is negative. And so, our perceptron implements a **NAND** gate!

The NAND example demonstrates that perceptrons can calculate any logical function since the NAND gate is a general-purpose computing device. This indicates that any calculation may be constructed using NAND gates.

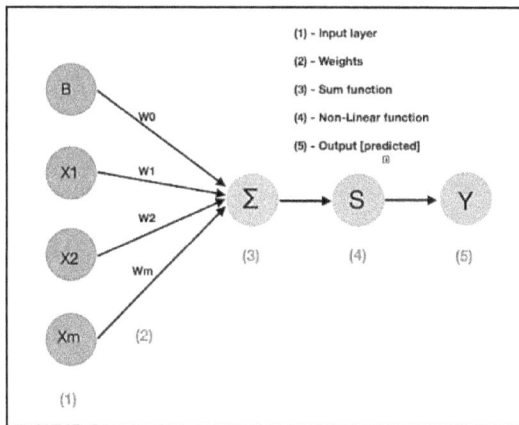

Figure 3: Data analysis with perceptron models makes use of an input layer, weights, and the SUM function.

The perceptron model has an input layer, weights for each unit, and a SUM function $[X1 * W1 + X2 * W2 + \cdots .. + XmWm]$ where

5

$X1\ X2\ ...\ Xm$ represents input features and $W1\ W2\ ...\ Wm$ represents weights, the projected output, followed by a non-linear function (as in **Figure 3**) about which more will be spoken. The following is written in mathematics as below:

$$\hat{y} = g\ (W0 + \sum Xi * Wi)$$
$$= g\ (W0 + X^T.W),$$
$$\text{Where, } X^T = [X1, ..., Xm] \& W = [W1, ..., Wm]^T$$

Each input is multiplied by its corresponding weight in a perceptron, which then takes the sum of all the inputs and passes it to a non-linear function to get a value between zero and one. As a result, the perceptron only activates if the net input is non-negative, *i.e.*,

$$output = w \cdot x + b \geq 0$$

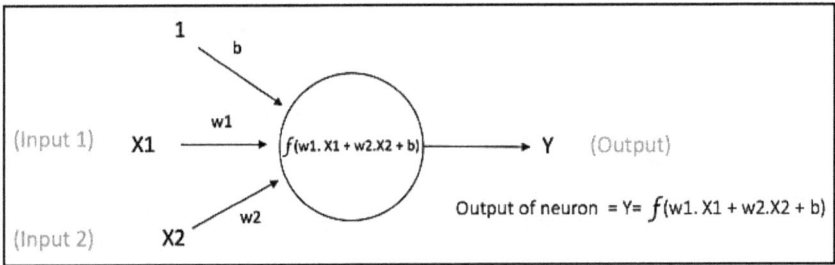

Figure 4: A single neuron.

Weights w1 and w2 are applied to the numerical inputs X1 and X2 of the **Figure 4** network. In addition, input 1 has a weight b (referred to as Bias) attached to it. As indicated in **Figure 4**, the neuron's output Y is calculated. The Activation Function, or f, is a non-linear function. Since most real-world data is nonlinear, this function adds nonlinearity to a neuron's output, which is significant.

Three non-linear functions are generally used **1. Sigmoid function, 2. Hyperbolic tangent, 3. Rectified Linear unit (ReLu)**. ReLU is a commonly used non-linear function in practice.

Non-linear functions allow for the approximation of complicated functions and improved predictions; linear functions do not since they yield linear judgements on data.

6

Importance of Bias: The primary purpose of Bias is to supply each node with a trainable constant value in addition to its usual inputs.

What are Neural Networks?

Numerous applications, including machine learning and artificial intelligence, employ neural networks. When you ask your mobile assistant to perform a search for you—say, **Google or Siri or Amazon Web**—or use a self-driving car, these are all neural network-driven [5]. Neural networks are systems with an input layer, many hidden layers, and an output layer that is modelled after the human brain. The neurons receive data as input and are sent to the following layer using the proper weights and biases. They are used in computer games and map programmes to adapt to players and discover the shortest route to their goal. The output is the final value predicted by the artificial neuron as in **Figure 5**.

A neural network's neurons are capable of many distinct functions:

- The weight of the channel that each input is multiplied by is discovered.
- The weighted sum, which is the sum of the weighted products, is calculated.
- The weighted total is increased by a neuron's bias value.
- Following that, the final total is put via a specific function called the activation function.

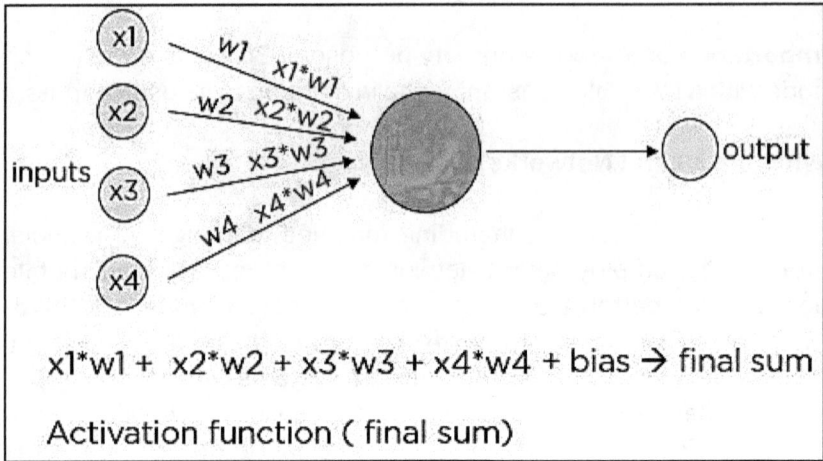

Figure 5: Data is fed as input to the neurons.

Introduction to Neural Network in Deep Learning

An artificial neural network (ANN) is a computational model that takes its cues from how biological neural networks function.

Biological Motivation and Connections

The basic computational unit of the brain is a neuron. Approximately 86 billion neurons can be found in the human nervous system, and they are connected with approximately $10^{14} - 10^{15}$ synapses. The **Figure 6** below shows a cartoon drawing of a biological neuron (left) and a common mathematical model (right).

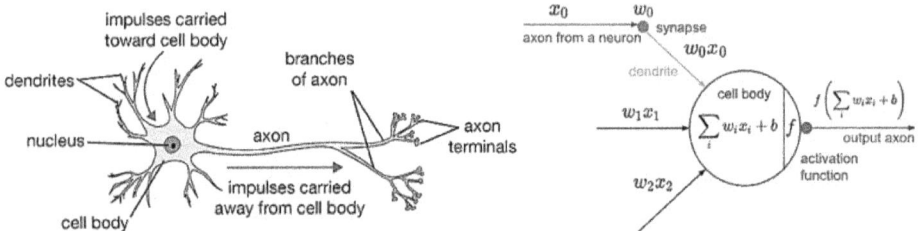

Figure 6: cartoon drawing of a biological neuron (left) and a common mathematical model (right).

The Perceptron Model

Using an artificial neural network that is modelled after how a neural system in the human body functions, the deep learning subfield of machine learning extracts more complex properties from data. A neural network is made up of numerous layers, each of which has multiple units. These layers are often divided into three categories: *1. An input layer, 2. Hidden layer(s), and 3. Output layer*. A weight (w) is applied to each input based on how significant it is in relation to other inputs. Each unit from one layer is linked to the following, creating a thick, layered neural network.

The junction between two neurons is called a **synapse**. The 7,000 synapses connecting neurons show the brain's tremendous degree of interconnectedness. The synaptic strength between these neurons is heightened as we discover new connections between concepts. This phenomenon is known as **Hebb's rule** (1949) that states "Cells that fire together wire together".

- **Neural networks**: Computers can learn from observational data using a biologically inspired programming paradigm.
- **Deep learning**, a powerful set of techniques for learning in neural networks.

For image identification, audio recognition, and natural language processing, neural networks and deep learning are the most effective technologies. Utilising a single neuron, binary classifiers may be developed.

Limitations of the Perceptron Model

Despite considerable progress, perceptrons are unable to learn basic operations like the XOR function as shown in **Figure 7.**

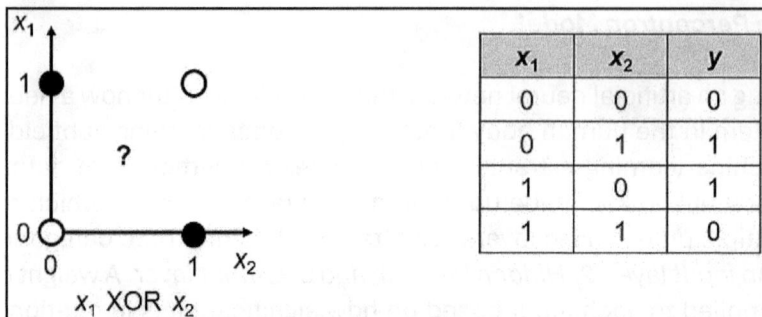

x_1	x_2	y
0	0	0
0	1	1
1	0	1
1	1	0

x_1 XOR x_2

Figure 7: The XOR problem cannot be solved by a perceptron.

Perceptrons cannot resolve the XOR issue because it is not linearly separable. However, more difficult, and non-linear issues can be resolved by layering numerous perceptrons [4].

The Architecture of a Neural Network

Neural networks are collections of neurons connected in an acyclic graph. The most common form of layer is a fully connected layer, in which neurons across two adjacent layers are pairwise coupled, but neurons within a single layer do not exchange connections. A stack of completely linked layers is used in two sample neural network topologies.

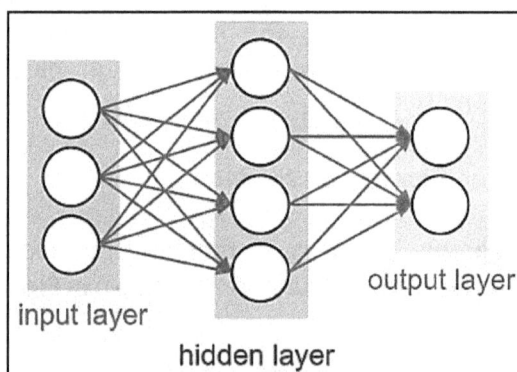

input layer

hidden layer

output layer

Figure 8: A 2-layer Neural Network (one hidden layer of 4 neurons (or units) and one output layer with 2 neurons), and three inputs.

10

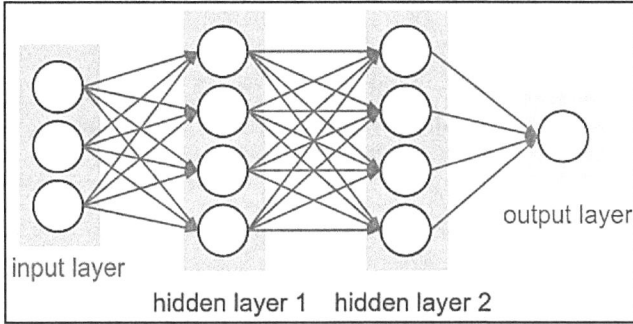

Figure 9: A 3-layer neural network with three inputs, two hidden layers of 4 neurons each and one output layer.

Synapses between neurons across layers exist, but not within a layer.

Input Nodes (input layer): This layer only passes information to the following one, which is frequently a buried layer, without doing any computations. Layer can also refer to a group of nodes.

Hidden Nodes (hidden layer): When performing intermediate processing or calculation, hidden layers transport the weights (signals or information) from the input layer to the subsequent layer (either another hidden layer or the output layer). A neural network can exist without a hidden layer.

Output Nodes (output layer): Here, we ultimately employ an activation function that corresponds to the desired output structure (for example, softmax for classification).

Connections and Weights: The *network* consists of connections, each connection transferring the output of a neuron i to the input of a neuron j. In this sense i is the predecessor of j and j is the successor of i, each connection is assigned a weight W_{ij}.

Activation Function: With respect to an input or group of inputs, a node's activation function determines the node's output. An ordinary computer chip circuit may be seen as a digital network of activation functions that, depending on input, are either "ON" (1) or

"OFF" (0). The linear perceptron in neural networks exhibits behaviour akin to this. In contrast, it is the nonlinear activation function that enables such networks to calculate nontrivial problems with a minimal number of nodes. This feature is referred to as the transfer function in artificial neural networks.

Learning Rule: The learning rule is a rule or method that adjusts the neural network's parameters such that a particular input will yield a preferred output. Usually, this learning process involves changing the weights and thresholds [6].

Sizing Neural Networks

Two metrics—the number of neurons and, more frequently, the number of parameters—are frequently used to gauge the scale of neural networks. Using **Figure 8** and **Figure 9** of the image above as examples, two networks are being studied.

The first network (left) has 4 + 2 = 6 neurons (not counting the inputs), [3 x 4] + [4 x 2] = 20 weights and 4 + 2 = 6 biases, for a total of 26 learnable parameters.

The second network (right) has 4 + 4 + 1 = 9 neurons, [3 x 4] + [4 x 4] + [4 x 1] = 12 + 16 + 4 = 32 weights and 4 + 4 + 1 = 9 biases, for a total of 41 learnable parameters.

Advantages of Neural Network

An autonomously debugging or diagnosing neural network called an ANN has the potential for great fault tolerance. If it can be automated, it can sift through and sort through thousands of log files from a corporation, saving time, energy, and resources. In the banking sector, for example, when employees work on a specific Excel file and gradually create codes around it, nonlinear systems might uncover shortcuts to computationally expensive solutions. ANN can provide the same results in a matter of seconds that it would take a major bank day, weeks, or even a month to complete.

Applications of Neural Network

Understanding the applications of artificial intelligence, machine learning, and neural networks is crucial since these technologies are employed more often.

Handwriting Recognition

Neural networks are used to convert handwritten characters into digital characters that a machine can recognize.

Stock-exchange Prediction

Numerous elements influence the stock market, making it challenging to monitor and comprehend. Stockbrokers might benefit from a neural network that can analyse these variables and anticipate the prices on a regular basis. However, the US stock exchange alone generates more than three terabytes of data every day, making it challenging to organise before focusing on a single firm.

Traveling Issues of Sales Professionals

Neural networks may assist in discovering the best travel routes for salespeople who are going from one area to another, but practical concerns must be taken into account.

Image Compression

To store, encrypt, and regenerate a picture, neural network data compression is utilised, which enables us to reduce data size and memory use.

How the Biological Model of Neural Networks Functions?

Electrochemical signals are sent by linked neurons in mammalian brains. Each neuron has a nucleus, dendrites, axons, and synapses that allow them to communicate with one another by passing information or impulses between them. The ~86 billion neurons in the human brain allow it to conduct a wide range of intricate tasks.

How Artificial Neural Networks Function?

Statistical models known as ANNs use learning algorithms to adapt and self-program. Developers set them up in layers that run concurrently. The input layer resembles the dendrites in the neural network of the human brain, while the hidden layer is between the input layer and output layer. A series of synaptic weight-based inputs are received by the hidden layer, which then uses a transfer function to send an output to the output layer. ANN Architecture shown in **Figure 10**.

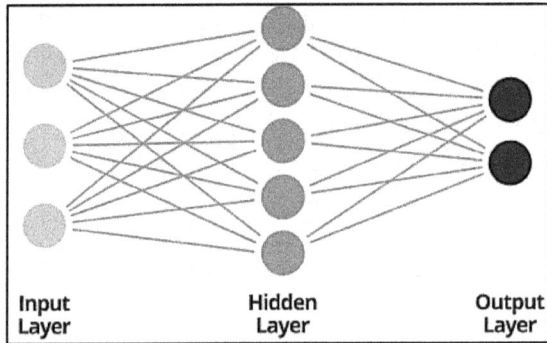

| Input
Layer | Hidden
Layer | Output
Layer |

Figure 10: ANN architecture.

How Do You Train a Neural Network?

As soon as a network is set up for a certain application, training (learning) may start. Unsupervised learning is the process through which a network learns to make sense of inputs on its own, as opposed to supervised learning, which produces desirable outputs by operator grading.

Why Do We Use Neural Networks?

Due to their human-like characteristics and versatility in job completion, neural networks are ideally suited for large data-based applications. In situations when there are no precise models available, they can also utilise regulated procedures to make sense of confusing, conflicting, or missing data [6].

Tasks Neural Networks Perform

Neural networks are useful because they can complete important tasks, including making sense of data, while preserving their other characteristics.

- Classification: NNs organize patterns or datasets into predefined classes.
- Prediction: They produce the expected output from given input.
- Clustering: They identify a unique feature of the data and classify it without any knowledge of prior data.
- Associating: Neuronal networks may be trained to always return to the version of a pattern that is closest to the unfamiliar version.

Deep learning, a collection of NN approaches used to tackle complex issues including bioinformatics, medication design, social network filtering, and natural language translation, relies on neural networks. The most challenging problems in science and engineering, including sophisticated robots, will be solved via deep learning. We progress regularly as neural networks get quicker and wiser.

Real-World and Industry Applications of Neural Networks

Neural networks, a subset of machine learning algorithms, have numerous real-world and industry applications [7]. Here are some notable examples:

Image and Speech Recognition: From face recognition to speech-to-text systems, virtual assistants, and self-driving cars, neural networks have revolutionised image and speech recognition.

Natural Language Processing (NLP): Since they can comprehend and produce human language, neural networks are crucial for NLP applications including sentiment analysis, language translation, Chabot, and text summarization.

Recommendation Systems: Businesses employ neural networks to personalise suggestions based on user preferences and behaviour, enhancing consumer engagement and satisfaction.

Financial Forecasting and Trading: Financial organisations employ neural networks to analyse massive amounts of data, spot trends, and make educated choices in areas including stock market forecasting, credit scoring, fraud detection, and algorithmic trading.

Healthcare and Medicine: For early diabetic identification, drug development, and individualised therapy recommendations, neural networks have demonstrated promise in the diagnosis of illnesses, patient outcomes prediction, and medical picture analysis [8, 9, 19].

Autonomous Vehicles: Self-driving vehicles cannot perceive their environment or make judgements without neural networks.

Robotics: Robots can recognise items, grip them, and manipulate them with the use of neural networks, which also help them navigate through challenging environments.

Financial Services and Fraud Detection: Banks and other financial organisations employ neural networks to spot fraudulent transactions, spot money laundering tendencies, and evaluate credit risk. They are able to spot irregularities and notify the appropriate authorities.

Energy and Utilities: Utilising neural networks may optimise the production of renewable energy sources, forecast power consumption, and enhance energy efficiency.

Manufacturing and Quality Control: In order to assure high-quality items, neural networks are employed to discover flaws in products and machinery by assessing sensor data, pictures, and sound patterns.

Many different sectors employ neural networks to promote creativity and boost productivity. AI will probably find more uses as it develops, stimulating creativity and enhancing productivity.

Current Examples of NN Business Applications

Here are further current examples of NN business applications [10]:

Banking: Loan delinquencies, fraud and risk assessment, credit and loan application review, and credit card attrition are all crucial.

Business Analytics: Market research, market mix, market structure, customer behaviour modelling, customer segmentation, fraud propensity, and models for attrition, default, buy, and renewals are crucial.

Defence: Face recognition, target tracking, feature extraction, noise reduction, object classification, sensors, sonar, and radar are some of the technologies used in counterterrorism.

Education: Adaptive learning software, dynamic forecasting, education system analysis and forecasting, student performance modelling [20], and personality profiling

Financial: Ratings of corporate bonds, financial analysis, credit line usage analysis, forecasting of currency prices, loan counselling, mortgage screening, appraisal, and portfolio trading.

Medical: Cancer cell analysis, ECG and EEG analysis, test recommendations for ERs, cost-saving measures, transplant procedure optimisation, and prosthetic design [8, 9].

Securities: Automatic bond rating, market analysis, and stock trading advisory systems

Transportation: Routing systems, truck brake diagnosis systems, and vehicle scheduling

Types of Neural Networks

In order to carry out the learning process, a training algorithm is necessary. Neural networks are algorithms that recognise patterns and interpret data. To accomplish various objectives, there are several training algorithms accessible [4].

Different Algorithms:

Autoencoder (AE)	Deep Belief Network (DBN)	Extreme Learning Machine (ELM)	Kohonen Network (KN)	Radial Basis Function Networks (RBF nets)
Bidirectional Recurrent Neural Network (BRNN)	Deep Convolutional Inverse Graphics Network (DCIGN)	Feed Forward Neural Network (FF or FFNN) and Perceptron (P)	Liquid State Machine (LSM)	Recurrent Neural Network (RNN)
Boltzmann Machine (BM)	Deep Residual Network (DRN)	Gated Recurrent Unit (GRU)	Long/Short-Term Memory (LSTM)	Restricted Boltzmann Machine (RBM)
Convolutional Neural Network (CNN)	Denoising Autoencoder (DAE)	Generative Adversarial Network (GAN)	Markov Chain (MC)	Support Vector Machine (SVM)
Deconvolutional Neural Network (DNN)	Echo State Network (ESN)	Hopfield Network (HN)	Neural Turing Machine (NTM)	Variational Autoencoder (VAE)

Neural Networks in Data Mining

Neural networks are non-linear statistical data modelling techniques used to detect patterns in data or describe complicated interactions between inputs and outputs. They are used by data warehousing companies to extract information from databases through the data mining process as in **Figure 11**.

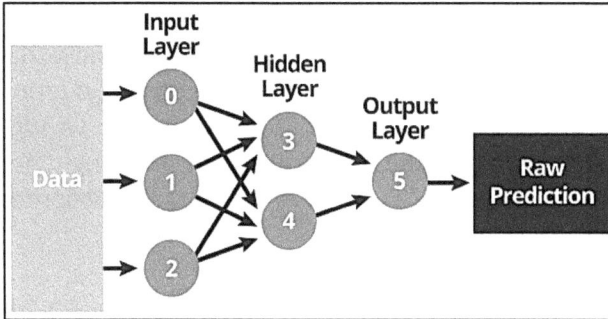

Figure 11: Neural networks in data mining.

Data warehouses allow for data modification and cross-fertilization, enabling users to make better informed judgements. Neural networks are not used to harvest data due to their long training periods and complex models.

Neural vs. Conventional Computers

Neural networks are able to perform tasks that conventional computers cannot, such as processing data consecutively, which are fundamental differences between traditional and neural computers.

- ***Following Instructions vs. Learning Capability:*** Neural networks are more advanced than conventional computers, which learn by carrying out steps or sequences. They are created to be more advanced, but their architecture limits them.
- ***Rules vs. Concepts and Imagery:*** Artificial neural networks use abstract concepts, visuals, and images to carry out tasks and learn from them, unlike conventional computers which follow rules.

The Challenges of Neural Networks

The value and implementation of neural networks depends on the task, so it's important to understand the challenges and limitations of each solution.

For instance, in Perfect Tense, we try to detect whether someone is using *a* or *an* correctly. In this case, using a neural network would be overkill, because you can simply look at the phonetic pronunciation to make the determination (*e.g.*, ***an banana*** is wrong). Neural networks are where most advances are being made right now. Things that were impossible only a year or two ago regarding content quality are now a reality.

Challenges in the Field of:

Training: For over-training on real-world tasks, neural networks are frequently criticised. The solution to this problem involves using a numerical optimisation approach and randomly rearranging training instances. Mini batches of examples are another strategy. For computer scientists, increasing training effectiveness and convergence capabilities is an active study subject.

Theoretical Issues: Facebook uses thousands of human reviewers since its algorithms can't detect all hate speech and false information. However, computers are unable to exhibit actual creativity, such as demonstrating mathematical theorems, making moral judgements, creating unique music, or innovating. AI and neural networks cannot solve this problem.

Inauthenticity: Although they are inspired by biological neural networks, artificial neural networks don't quite work like human brains. Statistical association, the foundation of artificial neural networks, is made possible by this mechanism. Because an ANN's learning process differs from a human's, it has inherent limits.

Hardware Issues: Because of the growth in computer power after 1991, neural networks have become a popular topic this century. Due to the utilisation of GPUs, training periods were shortened from months to days, enabling deeper learning and more multi-layering. To address rising computing needs, however, engineers require hardware advances as deep neural networks get more advanced. There are now being developed new hardware and processors for AI.

Using improved hardware and cross-pollinating various hardware and software, computer scientists and engineers are attempting to develop algorithms that are smarter, quicker, and more human-like.

The Future of Neural Networks

With numerous significant development areas in the works, neural networks are primed for immense potential:

Deep Learning Advances: In several fields, deep learning, a branch of neural networks, has produced outstanding achievements. Future developments in deep learning architectures, optimisation methods, and model interpretability could increase deep neural network performance, speed up training, and improve comprehension.

Reinforcement Learning: In robotics, autonomous systems, and gaming, reinforcement learning—which combines neural networks and trial-and-error learning—is gaining popularity. Future developments in algorithms and frameworks may result in more intelligent and flexible AI agents.

Explainable AI: Building confidence in AI systems, ensuring ethical usage, and facilitating regulatory compliance are all made possible by researchers' efforts to comprehend and explain how neural networks make decisions.

Neural Architecture Search: It is hoped that automating the architecture design process, known as neural architecture search (NAS), would lead to the creation of neural networks that are more effective, specialised, and domain specific.

Transfer Learning and Few-Shot Learning: Transfer learning enables neural networks to use information from one area to excel in another related one. Future research may concentrate on enhancing transfer learning capabilities, allowing neural networks to swiftly adapt to new tasks, and using less labelled data. The effectiveness of neural networks can also be increased through few-shot learning, which seeks to train models with less labelled input.

Neuromorphic Computing: Neuromorphic computing aims to create hardware that resembles biological brain networks, enabling faster and more energy-efficient calculations, opening up new possibilities for applications and deployment.

Ethical and Fair AI: Researchers and politicians are attempting to guarantee that AI technologies are created and applied ethically as neural networks are increasingly employed in important fields. Concerns including prejudice, justice, privacy, and responsibility are addressed in this.

Interdisciplinary Collaborations: Collaborations between academics and industry professionals can produce fresh ideas and methods for enhancing the functionality, interpretability, and usability of neural networks.

The future of artificial intelligence and machine learning will be shaped by neural networks, which offer enormous promise for improvements in performance, interpretability, and ethical issues.

Working of Neural Network

Three layers make up a neural network: the input layer, the hidden layer, and the output layer. While the hidden layer performs computations and feature extractions, the input layer gathers input signals and sends them to the next layer. The output layer provides the finished product, as shown in **Figure 12.**

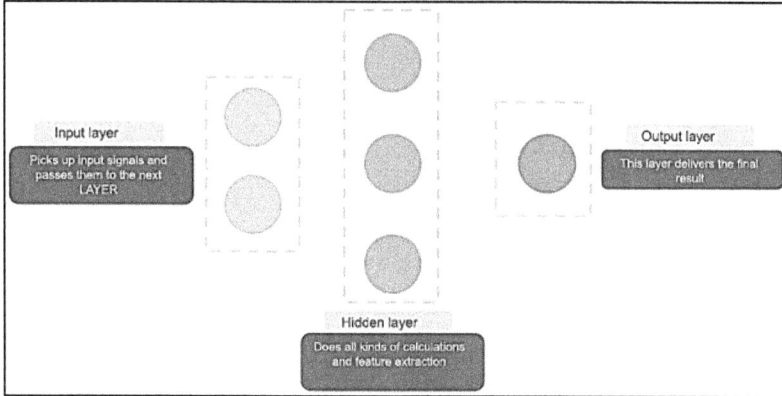

Figure 12: A neural network is usually described as having different layers.

Traffic cameras employ 28 by 28-pixel images to recognise licence plates and out-of-control automobiles. Each neuron has an activation number, which ranges from 0 to 1, that reflects the pixel's grayscale value. When a neuron's activity comes near to 1, it lights up.

Arrays of pixels are delivered into the input layer. Since you cannot alter the size of the input layer, if your picture is more than 28 by 28 pixels, you must reduce its size. We'll refer to the inputs in our case as X1, X2, and X3 in **Figure 13**. Each of those corresponds to one of the incoming pixels. The input is subsequently sent from the input layer to the concealed layer. Weights are distributed at random across the links. The input signal is multiplied by the weights, and a bias is applied to each of them.

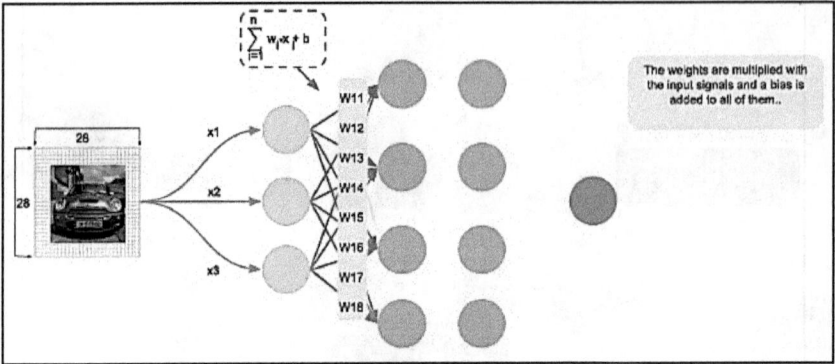

The weights are multiplied with the input signals and a bias is added to all of them..

Figure 13: Real-life example of how traffic cameras identify license plates and speeding vehicles on the road.

The activation function in each layer receives the weighted total of inputs to determine which nodes to fire for feature extraction. **Figure 14** illustrates this.

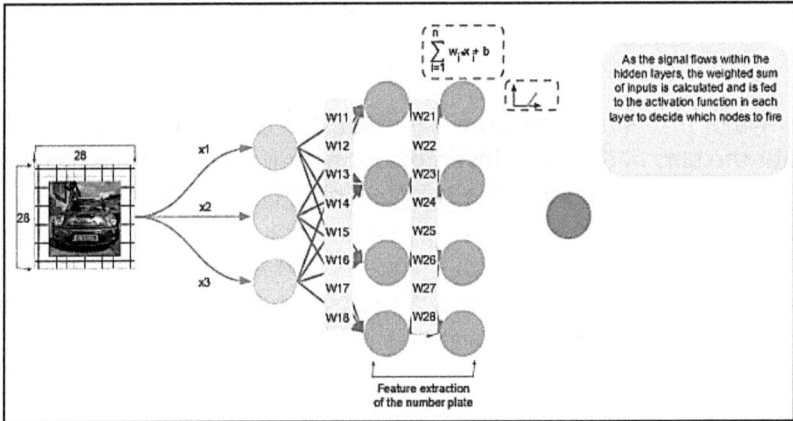

As the signal flows within the hidden layers, the weighted sum of inputs is calculated and is fed to the activation function in each layer to decide which nodes to fire

Feature extraction
of the number plate

Figure 14: The weighted sum of inputs is calculated and fed to the activation function in each layer to decide which nodes to fire.

Next, we'll take a detour to examine the neural network *activation function*. There are several types of activation functions.

What is an Activation Function and Why Use Them?

The activation function is used to provide nonlinearity to a neuron's output [7]. In a neural network, the weights and biases of the neurons are adjusted based on the output error. **Back-propagation** is made feasible by activation functions since they supply gradients together with the error to update the weights and biases. The activation function converts the output values into the appropriate range, such as between 0 and 1 or −1 and 1. For instance, the logistic activation function would convert all inputs in the real number domain into a range between 0 and 1.

Example of a Binary Classification Problem:

A binary classification issue asks if an input x, such as a picture, has the right object or not. A 1 is given if the object is correct; otherwise, a 0 is given. A binary classification issue might look something like this.

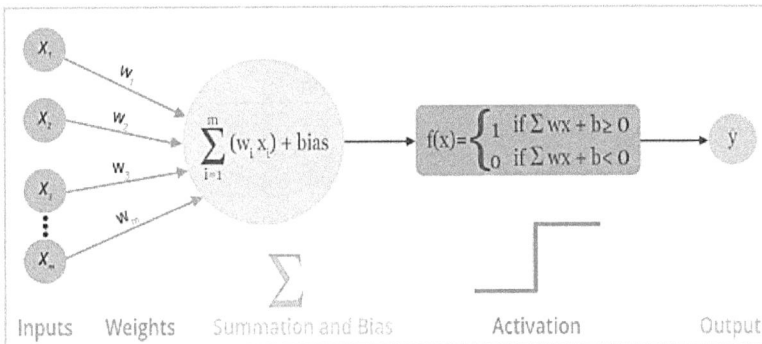

Figure 15: Multiply each of the features with a weight and sum them all together.

When we multiply each of the features with a weight (w1, w2, ..., wm) and sum them all together,
$Node\ output\ =\ activation\ (weighted\ sum\ of\ inputs),$ as in
Figure 15.

$$W.X = w1.x1 + w2.x2 + w3.x3 + \cdots \ldots \ldots \ldots + wn.xn = \sum_{i=1}^{m} w1.x1$$

25

Why Do We Need Non-linear Activation Function?

Without an activation function, a neural network is just a linear regression model. An activation function applies a non-linear adjustment to the input to enable learning and increasingly difficult tasks [2]. Even after including a hidden layer, a neural network without an activation function will still produce a linear function. It is essential to have an activation function because a non-linear activation function will enable the neuron to learn according to the difference in error.

Different Types of Activation Functions

The Activation Functions are basically two types:

Linear Activation Function – as shown in **Figure 16**.

$$\text{Equation:} f(x) = x$$

$$\text{Range:} (-infinity \ to \ infinity)$$

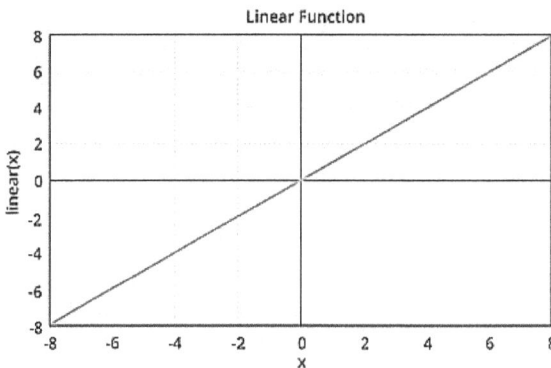

Figure 16: Linear activation function.

Non-linear Activation Functions

Non-linear Activation Functions (ReLUs) are used to generalise with a range of inputs and distinguish between outcomes. ReLUs are substantially quicker for bigger networks, according to simulations.

When an output is non-linear, a linear combination of inputs cannot recreate it. **Figure 17** displays non-linear activation functions.

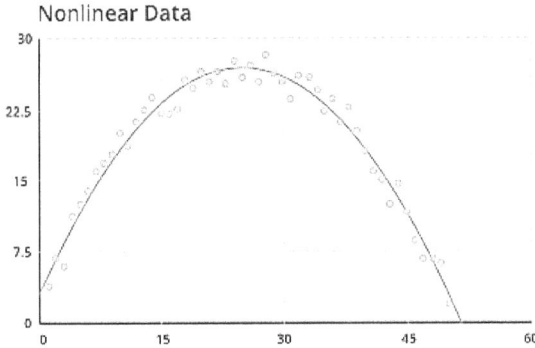

Nonlinear Data

Figure 17: Non-linear activation functions.

The Nonlinear Activation Functions are mainly divided on the basis of their range or curves.

For example: Regression analysis is used to determine a home's price, with linear activation at the output layer and non-linear function at hidden levels.

Sigmoid Function

- It is a function which is plotted as **'S'** shaped graph.
- **Equation:** $A = 1/(1 + e^{-x})$
- **Nature:** Non-linear. Observe that while Y values are quite steep, X values range from -2 to 2. This implies that tiny changes in x would likewise result in significant changes in the value of Y.
- **Value Range:** 0 to 1
- **Uses:** Sigmoid functions are frequently employed in binary classification output layers because their values only fall between 0 and 1, making it simple to anticipate that the outcome will be 1 if the value is larger than 0.5 and 0 otherwise.

Tanh or Hyperbolic Tangent Function

- The activation that works almost always better than sigmoid function is *Tanh* function also known as **Tangent Hyperbolic function** as in **Figure 18**. It's essentially a sigmoid function that has been mathematically shifted. Both are comparable to and derivable from one another.
- **Equation:**

$$f(x) = \tanh x = \frac{2}{1 + e^{-2x}} - 1$$

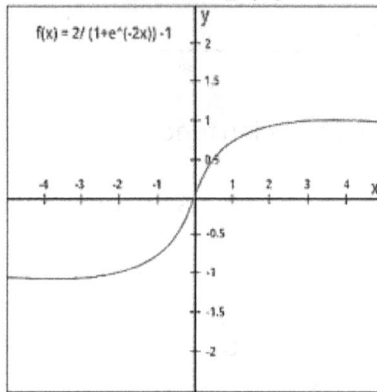

Figure 18: hyperbolic tangent function.

- **Value Range:** $-1\ to\ +1$
- **Nature:** non-linear
- **Uses: -** As its values typically range from -1 to 1, the mean for the hidden layer of a neural network will be 0 or near to it. This helps to centre the data by bringing the mean close to 0. This greatly simplifies learning for the subsequent layer.

RELU Function

- It Stands for *Rectified linear unit* shown in **Figure 19**. It is the most widely used activation function. Chiefly implemented in *hidden layers* of neural network.
- **Equation:** $A(x) = max\ (0, x)$. It gives an output x if x is positive and 0 otherwise.

- **Value Range:** $[0, inf)$
- **Nature:** Since the ReLU function is non-linear, it is simple to back propagate mistakes and activate several layers of neurons.

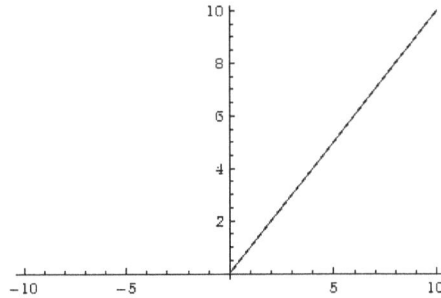

Figure 19: RELU rectified linear unit.

- **Uses:** ReLu requires fewer mathematical processes than $tanh$ and sigmoid, making it less computationally costly. Only a small number of neurons are active at once, making the network sparse and effective for computing.

In simple words, RELU learns *much faster* than *sigmoid* and *tanh* function.

Softmax Function

The softmax function, as seen in **Figure 20**, is a subtype of the sigmoid function and is useful for dealing with multi-class classification issues.

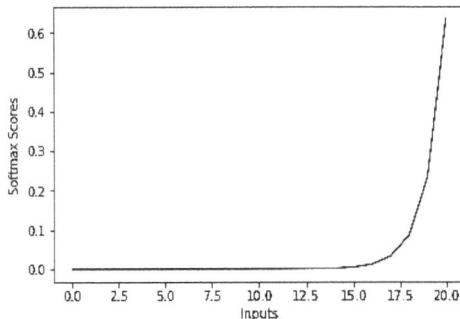

Figure 20: Softmax function.

- **Nature:** non-linear
- **Uses:** Usually employed when managing several classes. The output layer of image classification issues frequently contained the softmax algorithm. The softmax function would divide by the total outputs while simultaneously squeezing each class's outputs into a range between 0 and 1.
- **Output:** The softmax function is ideally used in the output layer of the classifier where we are actually trying to attain the *probabilities* to define the class of each input.

The Rule of Thumb:

- The basic rule of thumb is if you really don't know what activation function to use, then simply use **RELU** as it is a general activation function in *hidden layers* and is used in most cases these days.
- If your output is for *binary* classification then, *sigmoid* function is very natural choice for output layer.
- If your output is for *multi-class* classification then, *Softmax* is particularly useful to predict the probabilities of each class.

Types of Neural Networks

The different types of neural networks as shown in **Figure 21** are discussed below:

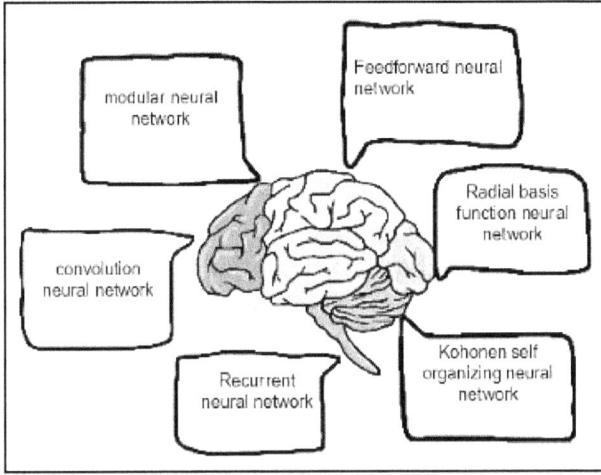

Figure 21: Different types of neural networks.

I.   Feed-forward Neural Network

An artificial neural network known as an ANN (artificial neural network) solely moves from input to output. It takes some time to train but is rapid when utilised in *voice* and *visual recognition* applications.

II.   Radial Basis Functions Neural Network

For the purpose of *power restoration systems*, this model categorises data points depending on how far they are from a central point. It searches for related data points and organises them.

III.   Kohonen Self-organizing Neural Network

Vectors of random input are input to a discrete map comprised of neurons. Vectors are also called dimensions or planes. Applications include using it to **recognize patterns** in data like a **medical** analysis.

IV.   Recurrent Neural Network

In this type, the hidden layer saves its output to be used for future prediction. The output becomes part of its new input. Applications include **text-to-speech conversion**.

V. Convolution Neural Network

In this type, the input features are taken in batches—as if they pass through a filter. This allows the network to remember an image in parts. Applications include signal and image processing, such as *facial recognition*.

VI. Modular Neural Network

This is composed of a collection of different neural networks working together to get the output. This is innovative and is still in the research phase.

Implementation of Perceptron Algorithm for OR Logic Gate with 2-bit Binary Input

OR logical function truth table for 2-bit binary variables are as in **Table 1**:

Table 1: OR-truth table for 2-bit binary variables

X1	X2	y
0	0	0
0	1	1
1	0	1
1	1	1

Now for the corresponding weight vector w: $(w1, w2)$ of the input vector x: $(x1, x2)$, the associated Perceptron (as in **Figure 22**) Function can be defined as: $\hat{y} = \theta(w1x1 + w2x2 + b)$

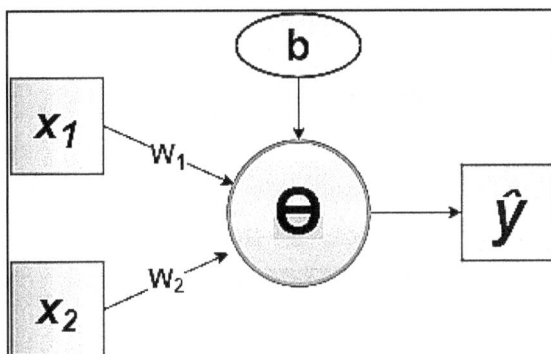

Figure 22: Perceptron for input vector x: $(x1, x2)$ and weight vector w: $(w1, w2)$.

For the implementation, considered weight parameters are $w1 = 1$, $w2 = 1$ and the bias parameter is $b = -0.5$

Python Implementation:

```python
# importing Python library
import numpy as np

# define Unit Step Function
def unitStep(v):
    if v >= 0:
        return 1
    else:
        return 0

# design Perceptron Model
def perceptronModel(x, w, b):
    v = np.dot(w, x) + b
    y = unitStep(v)
    return y

# OR Logic Function
# w1 = 1, w2 = 1, b = -0.5
def OR_logicFunction(x):
    w = np.array([1, 1])
    b = -0.5
    return perceptronModel(x, w, b)

# testing the Perceptron Model
test1 = np.array([0, 1])
test2 = np.array([1, 1])
test3 = np.array([0, 0])
test4 = np.array([1, 0])

print("OR({}, {}) = {}".format(0, 1, OR_logicFunction(test1)))
print("OR({}, {}) = {}".format(1, 1, OR_logicFunction(test2)))
print("OR({}, {}) = {}".format(0, 0, OR_logicFunction(test3)))
print("OR({}, {}) = {}".format(1, 0, OR_logicFunction(test4)))
```

Output:
> OR (0, 1) = 1
> OR (1, 1) = 1
> OR (0, 0) = 0
> OR (1, 0) = 1

According to the truth table for 2-bit binary input, the model's projected output (y hat) for each test input matches the OR logic gate's conventional output (y), demonstrating the effectiveness of the perceptron technique for OR logic gates.

Multi-Layer Perceptrons: Notations and Trainable Parameters

The inability of single layer perceptrons to capture non-linearity in non-linear input is an issue that can be readily resolved by multi-layer perception.

A multi-layer perceptron consists of input and output layers as well as one or more hidden layers that each include several neurons layered on top of one another. Any arbitrary activation function may be used, as well as activation functions that enforce thresholds like ReLU or sigmoid. The more hidden layers and nodes there are, the better the findings are at capturing the non-linear behaviour of the dataset [2].

MLP Notations

The back-propagation technique, which trains a neural network to iteratively update weights and biases and achieve the best accuracy, is one of the most crucial elements. In neural networks, weights and biases may be learned.

For a neural network to be trained, back-propagation, a process of updating weights and biases, is necessary.

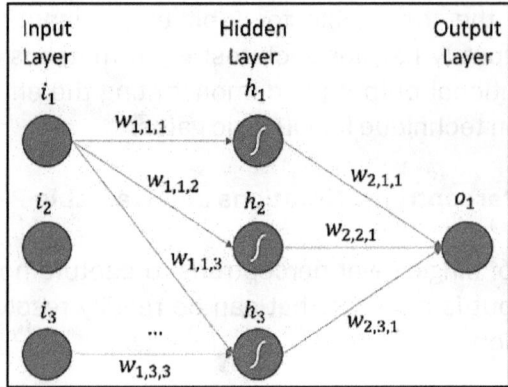

Figure 23: Multi-layer neural network.

The above **Figure 23** shows the multi-layer neural network having an input layer, a hidden layer, and an output layer.

Notation for Weights:

Notation: W_{ij}^h

Where,
$i = $ *From which node weight is passing to the next layer's node.*
$j = $ *To which node weight is arriving.*
$h = $ *Layer in which weight is arriving.*

Example:

W_{11}^1
= Weight passing into 1st node of 1st layer of 1st node of the previous layer.

W_{23}^1
= Weight passing into the 3rd node of the 1st hidden layer from the 2nd node of the previous layer

W_{45}^1
= Weight passing into the 5th node of the 2nd hidden layer from the 4th node of the previous layer.

Notations for Biases:

Notation: b_{ij}

Where,
$i = Layer\ to\ which\ a\ bias\ belongs.$
$j = node\ to\ which\ a\ bias\ belongs.$

Example:

$b_{11} = biases\ of\ 1st\ node\ of\ 1st\ hidden\ layer.$
$b_{23} = bias\ of\ 3rd\ of\ 2nd\ hidden\ layer.$
$b_{41} = bias\ of\ 1st\ node\ of\ 4th\ hidden\ layer.$

Notations for Outputs:

Notation: O_{ij}

Where,
$i = Layer\ to\ which\ a\ bias\ belongs.$
$j = node\ to\ which\ a\ bias\ belongs.$

Example:

$O_{11} = Output\ of\ 1st\ node\ of\ 1st\ hidden\ layer.$
$O_{45} = Output\ of\ 5th\ of\ 4th\ hidden\ layer.$
$O_{34} = Output\ of\ 4th\ node\ of\ 3rd\ hidden\ layer.$

Calculating Total Trainable Parameters

Total Trainable Parameters for a given between 2 layers of an artificial neural network is a sum of total weights and total biases that exist between them.

Total Trainable Parameters Between two layers in a Neural Network

$$= [\ Number\ of\ Nodes\ in\ the\ first\ layer$$
$$*\ Number\ of\ nodes\ in\ the\ second\ layer\ ](Weights)$$
$$+\ [\ Number\ of\ nodes\ in\ the\ second\ layer\ ](Biases)$$

1. Trainable Parameters between the Input layer and First Hidden Layer:

$weights = 3 * 4 = 12$
$biases = 4 \ (4 \ nodes \ in \ 1st \ hidden \ layer)$
$Trainable \ Parameters = weights + biases$
$= 12 + 4$
$= 16$

2. Trainable Parameters between First Hidden layer and Second Hidden Layer:

$weights = 4 * 2 = 8$
$biases = 2 \ (2 \ nodes \ in \ 1st \ hidden \ layer)$
$Trainable \ Parameters = weights + biases$
$= 8 + 2$
$= 10$

3. Trainable Parameters between Second Hidden layer and Output Layer:

$weights = 2 * 2 = 4$
$biases = 2 \ (2 \ nodes \ in \ 1st \ hidden \ layer)$
$Trainable \ Parameters = weights + biases$
$= 4 + 2$
$= 6$

Training our MLP: The Back-Propagation Algorithm

Let's take an example to understand Multi-Layer Perceptrons better. Suppose we have the following student-marks dataset:

Hours Studied	Midterm Marks	Final Term Result
35	67	1 (Pass)
12	75	0 (Fail)
16	89	1 (Pass)
45	56	1 (Pass)
10	90	0 (Fail)

The student's study hours and midterm grade are displayed in the two input columns. The last Result column might have a value of 1 or 0, indicating whether the student passed the last term. For instance, a student would pass the final term if they put in 35 hours of study and received 67 on their midterm.

Now, suppose, we want to predict whether a student studying 25 hours and having 70 marks in the midterm will pass the final term.

Hours Studied	Midterm Marks	Final Term Result
25	70	?

Informed predictions may be made by a multi-layer perceptron given a fresh data point after learning from training data. How it learns these correlations will be demonstrated.

The process by which a Multi-Layer Perceptron learns is called the **Back propagation algorithm**.

Backward Propagation of Errors is one of the several ways in which an artificial neural network (ANN) can be trained. It is a supervised training scheme, which means, it learns from labelled training data (there is a supervisor, to guide its learning).

To put in simple terms, *Back Propagation* is like **"learning from mistakes."** The supervisor **corrects** the ANN whenever it makes mistakes.

In order to calculate the output vector from an input vector, learning entails giving the appropriate weights to connections between nodes in adjacent layers. In supervised learning, the training set is labelled, indicating that the desired/expected outcome is known for certain provided inputs.

Backward Propagation Algorithm:

At first, all edge weights are allocated at random. The ANN is triggered, and its output is scrutinised, for each input in the training dataset. The mistake is "propagated" back to the top layer after comparison with the expected result, which we already know. The weights are "adjusted" in response when this inaccuracy is discovered. The output error is then repeated in this manner until it falls below a predefined threshold [2, 7].

We have a "learned" ANN when the aforementioned algorithm finishes running, and we consider it to be prepared to work with "new" inputs. It is claimed that this ANN has learnt from both its faults (error propagation) and multiple instances (labelled data). Let's come back to our student-marks dataset shown above.

The input layer of the multilayer perceptron in **Figure 24** comprises two nodes: one for hours studied and one for midterm marks. Another layer, which is concealed, has two nodes: one for success and one for failure. There are two nodes in the output layer: one for success and one for failure.

To guarantee that the outputs are probabilities that sum up to 1, the Softmax function is employed as the Activation Function in the Multi-Layer Perceptron's Output layer. It reduces a vector of arbitrary real-valued scores to a vector of sum able values between zero and one. So, in this case,

$$Probability\ (Pass)\ +\ Probability\ (Fail)\ =\ 1$$

Step 1: *Forward Propagation*

The network's weights are all allocated at random. Think about the hidden layer node designated V in Figure 5 below. Assume that the connections from the inputs to that node have the weights w1, w2, and w3 (see **Figure 24**).

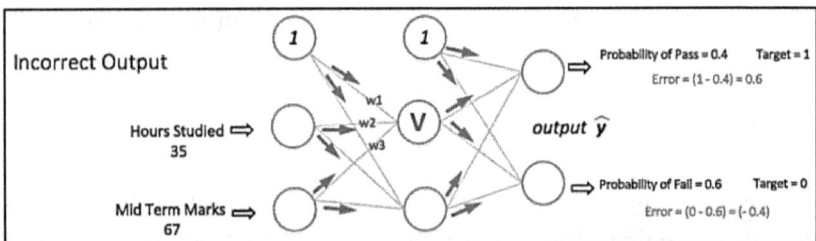

Figure 24: Forward propagation step in a multi-layer perceptron.

The network then takes the first training example as input (we know that for inputs 35 and 67, the probability of Pass is 1).
Input to the network $= [35, 67]$

Desired output from the network (target) $= [1, 0]$
Then output V from the node in consideration can be calculated as below (f is an activation function such as sigmoid):

$$V = f(1 * w1 + 35 * w2 + 67 * w3)$$

The two nodes in the output layer get information from the two nodes in the hidden layer, enabling them to determine output probabilities. The network in Figure 24 is considered to have an "*Incorrect Output*" since the computed probabilities (0.4 and 0.6) are significantly different from the required probability (1 and 0, respectively).

Step 2: *Back Propagation and Weight Updating*

We calculate the **total error** at the output nodes and propagate these errors *back* through the network using Back propagation to calculate the **gradients**.

Then we use an **optimization method** such as **Gradient Descent** to 'adjust' all weights in the network with an aim of *reducing the error* at the output layer. This is shown in the **Figure 25** below.

Suppose that the new weights associated with the node in consideration are w4, w5 and w6 (after Back propagation and adjusting weights).

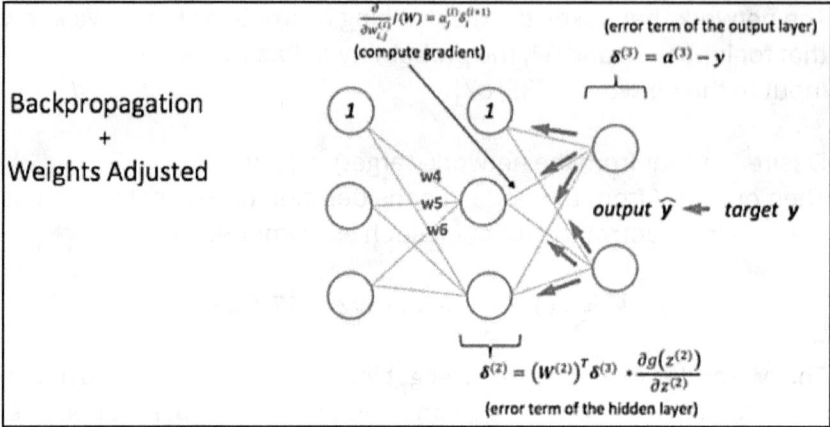

Figure 25: Step for updating weights and propagating backwards in a multi-layer perceptron.

The network should perform better if we feed it the same example again because the weights have been modified to reduce prediction error. As shown in **Figure 26**, the errors at the output nodes now reduce to $[0.2, -0.2]$ as compared to $[0.6, -0.4]$ earlier. This demonstrates that our network has learned to correctly categorise the first training case.

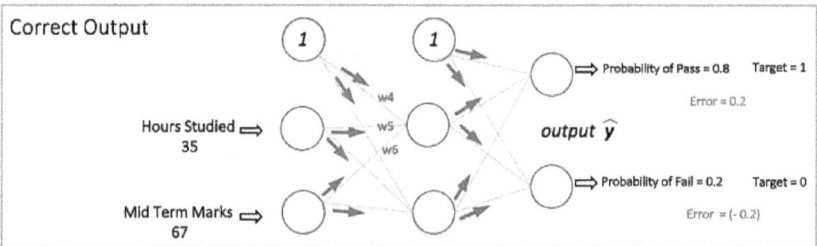

Figure 26: The MLP network now performs better on the same input.

All additional training instances in our dataset are used to repeat this procedure. Our network is claimed to have learned such examples after that.

Prediction: We utilise forward propagation to determine if a student who studies 25 hours and received 70 on the midterm will pass the final term. Calculated are the Pass and Fail output probabilities.

Problem with Back Propagation

Back propagation enables us to train neural networks efficiently, but when we employ more layers, the performance degrades and occasionally becomes impossible owing to disappearing or exploding gradients brought on by the repetitive computation of gradients using the chain rule.

Vanishing Gradients

When a gradient is multiplied by a quantity less than one, it disappears, becoming infinitesimally tiny. As a result, we are unable to place our loss function in the ideal state, resulting in the step size approaching zero.

Exploding Gradients

The network may become unstable if the gradient is multiplied by a number greater than one. NaN values, which are undefined values rather than numbers, may result from this.

Deep Learning Platforms

Now we will learn about several deep learning platforms and when they are used.

- **Torch:** Torch was developed using LUA and C, and its Python implementation is PyTorch.
- **Keras:** Keras is a Python framework for deep learning with reusability of code for CPU and GPU.
- **TensorFlow:** TensorFlow is an open-source deep-learning library developed by Google, which can be run on top of Keras.

- **DL4J:** Deep Learning for Java (DL4J), is the first deep learning library written for Java and Scala, integrated with Hadoop and Spark.

The most widely used learning library worldwide right now is Google's TensorFlow. Tensors, which are n-dimensional vectors or matrices, serve as its foundation [2, 4, 7].

Deep Learning Applications Used Across Industries

Virtual Assistants	Chatbots	Healthcare	Entertainment	News Aggregation and Fake News Detection
Composing Music	Image Colouring	Robotics	Image Captioning	Advertising
Self-Driving Cars	Natural Language Processing	Visual Recognition	Fraud Detection	Personalisation
Detecting Developmental Delay in Children	Colourisation of Black and White images	Adding Sounds to Silent Movies	Automatic Machine Translation	Automatic Handwriting Generation
Automatic Game Playing	Language Translations	Pixel Restoration	Demographic and Election Predictions	Green Smart Home Automation [21]

What is Neural Computing?

Artificial neural networks (ANNs) are used in neural computing to mimic the operation and behaviour of biological neural networks in the brain. ANNs are machine learning models made up of linked nodes that may learn to recognise patterns and make predictions based on input data. Large datasets are used to train ANNs, which entails modifying the weights and biases of the neurons to reduce the error between expected and actual output data.

With the development of machine learning and deep learning techniques, neural computing has emerged as a significant area of artificial intelligence study. Natural language processing, predictive modelling, and picture and audio recognition are some applications in industries including engineering, finance, and healthcare. Advancements in deep learning and machine learning methodologies have resulted from it.

Types of Neural Computing?

There are several types of neural computing, each with its own unique architecture and applications. Here are some of the most common types [6]:

I.   **Feed forward neural networks:** An input layer, an output layer, and one or more hidden layers are the basic components of a neural network. The network processes data as it is taught to spot patterns in the input data and generate the matching output.

II. **Recurrent neural networks:** With loops that allow information to be transmitted from one time step to the next and the ability to recognise temporal patterns in input data, networks are built to handle sequential data.

III. **Convolutional neural networks:** Convolutional networks are used in image and video processing to identify patterns in spatial data by learning features at various levels of abstraction using convolutional layers. In pictures, they can also spot patterns and items.

IV. **Auto encoders:** The encoder and decoder in unsupervised learning networks are taught to recreate the input data from a lower-dimensional representation. For dimensionality reduction and feature extraction, auto encoders are employed.

V.   **Deep belief networks:** For applications like speech and picture recognition, Boltzmann machines are unsupervised learning algorithms that can learn to recognise intricate patterns in input data.

There are several types and structures utilised in the difficult subject of neural computing.

How Neural Computing Works?

Artificial neural networks (ANNs) are used in neural computing to mimic the behaviour and operation of organic neural networks in the brain. Interconnected nodes that can learn to recognise patterns and anticipate outcomes make up ANNs.

Here's a general overview of how neural computing works:

a) Data is sent into a neural network typically as a matrix or vector.
b) Each artificial neuron in the network processes the input data mathematically as it passes the data through.
c) Each neuron's output is then sent to the layer of neurons below, where the cycle is continued until the output layer is reached.
d) In order to reduce the error between expected and actual output data, the neurons' weights and biases are changed during training.
e) Using methods like regularisation, dropout, and hyper parameter tuning, the neural network may be further optimised and fine-tuned to better categorise new data or make predictions based on the learnt patterns.

With applications in audio and image identification, natural language processing, and predictive modelling, neural computing is a potent machine learning tool. Its efficacy is influenced by the network design, training optimisation techniques, and the quality of the training data.

Difference Between Neural Network and Neural Computing

Although they are connected, neural networks and neural computing are two distinct ideas. A neural network is a type of machine learning model that consists of linked nodes, or synthetic neurons, which can learn to identify patterns and predict outcomes based on input data. The use of artificial neural networks (ANNs) to mimic the behaviour of biological neural networks in the brain falls under the wider category of neural computing. Neural computing encompasses not only the use of neural networks but also various kinds of models and algorithms that draw inspiration from the composition and operation of the human brain.

A particular kind of machine learning model that is a subset of neural computing is called a neural network. Neural networks, genetic algorithms, fuzzy logic, and swarm intelligence are just a few examples of the models and methods that fall under the umbrella term "neural computing," which includes a far wider variety of concepts. A larger subject known as "neural computing" encompasses a number of models and methods that are based on the structure and operation of the brain.

Introduction to Convolutional Neural Networks (ConvNets or CNNs)

Convolutional neural networks were invented by Yann Le Cun, who created the first LeNet in 1988. Originally utilised for character recognition tasks like reading zip codes and numbers, LeNet is currently employed in the healthcare industry for facial identification, object detection, and illness diagnosis. The basis of facial recognition, object identification, and illness diagnosis is convolutional neural networks (CNNs) [10, 11]. *Here's an example of convolutional neural networks that illustrates how they work:*

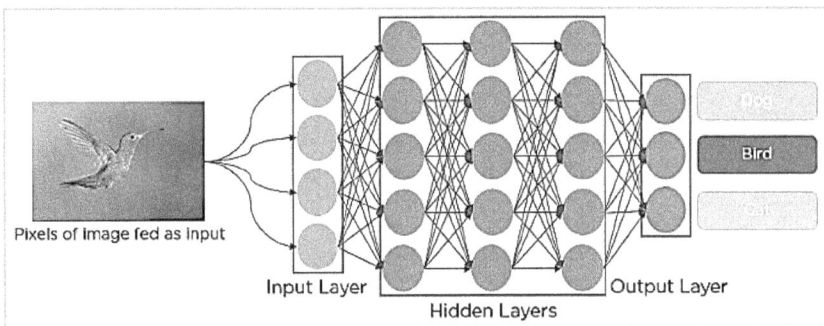

Figure 27: Convolutional Neural Network to identify the image of a bird.

Think about trying to determine whether a picture of a bird is indeed a bird or another item. As shown in **Figure 27**, you start by feeding the input layer of the neural network (a multi-layer network used to categorise objects) with the picture's pixels in the form of arrays. Every image may be represented as a matrix of pixel values. By executing various computations and manipulations, the hidden layers carry out feature extraction. Several hidden layers, including the convolution layer, the ReLU layer, and the pooling layer, extract features from the picture. The item in the picture is finally identified by a completely linked layer.

What is Convolutional Neural Network?

A feed-forward neural network called a convolutional network analyses visual picture by processing data in a grid-like architecture. It is used to find and categorise items in images, which are shown as an array of pixel values in **Figure 28**.

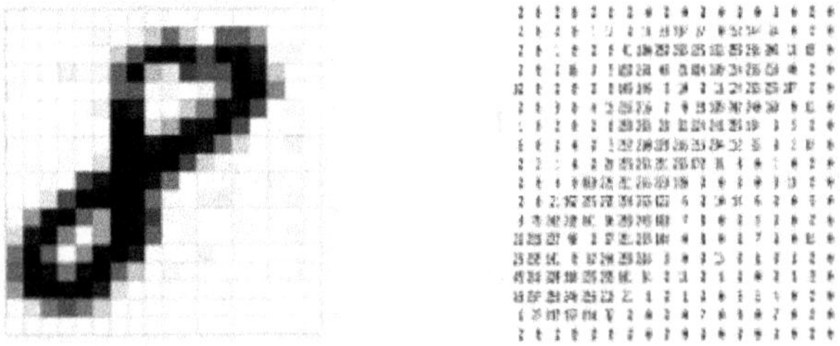

Figure 28: Every image is a matrix of pixel values.

The *convolution operation* forms the basis of any convolutional neural network. As we discussed above, every image can be considered as a matrix of pixel values. Consider a 5 X 5 image whose pixel values are only 0 and 1 (note that for a grayscale image, pixel values range from 0 to 255, the ***green*** matrix below is a special case where pixel values are only 0 and 1). Also, consider another 3 X 3 ***orange*** matrix as shown in **Figure 29**:

Figure 29: 5 X 5 and 3 X 3 Image Matrix of pixel values with only 0 and 1.

Then, the Convolution of the 5 x 5 image and the 3 x 3 matrix can be computed as shown in the animation in **Figure 30** below:

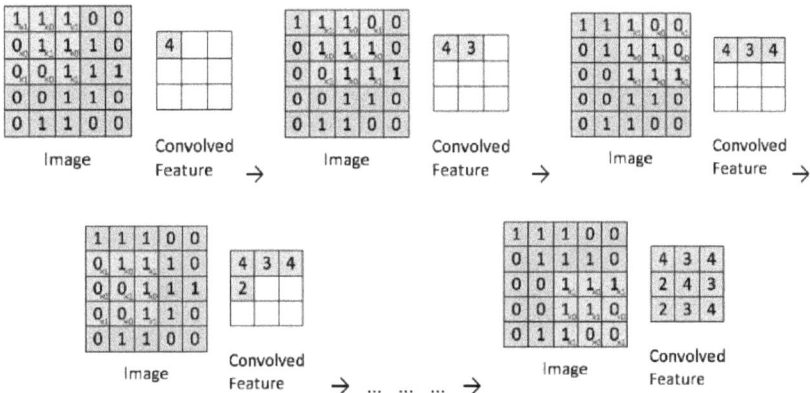

Figure 30: The Convolution operation. The output matrix is called convolved feature or feature map.

Now how the computation above (in **Figure 30**) is being done? We slide the *orange* matrix over our original image (*green*) by 1 pixel (also called '*stride*') and for every position, we compute element wise multiplication (between the two matrices) and add the multiplication outputs to get the final integer which forms a single element of the output matrix (*pink*). Note that the 3×3 matrix "sees" only a part of the input image in each *stride*.

In CNN terminology, the 3×3 matrix is called a '*filter*' or '*kernel*' or 'feature detector' and the matrix formed by sliding the filter over the image and computing the dot product is called the 'Convolved

49

Feature' or 'Activation Map' or the **'Feature Map'**. It is important to note that filters act as feature detectors from the original input image.

It is evident from the above that different values of the **filter matrix** will produce different **Feature Maps** for the same input image.
In practice, a CNN learns the values of these **filters** on its own during the training process (although we still need to specify parameters such as **number of filters, filter size, architecture of the network** etc. before the training process). The greater number of filters we have, the more image features get extracted and the better our network becomes at recognizing patterns in unseen images [10, 11].

What is Meant by Feature Maps in Convolutional Neural Networks?

The number of feature maps in **Figure 31** corresponds to the number of filters (kernel) applied to the input. Only the required properties of the input may pass through filters, which function similarly to membranes.

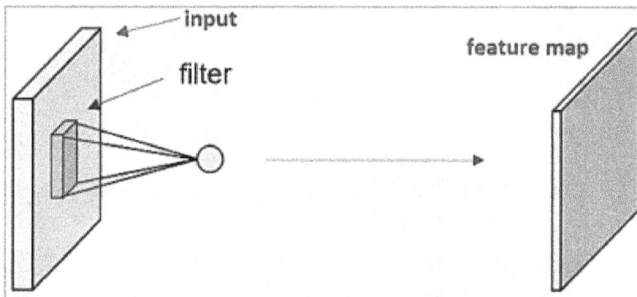

Figure 31: Feature maps.

Here in **Figure 32** the 3 × 3 matrix is called a **'filter'** or **'convolution kernel'** or 'feature detector' and the matrix formed by sliding the filter over the image and computing the dot product is called the 'Convolved Feature' or 'Activation Map' or the **'Feature Map'**.

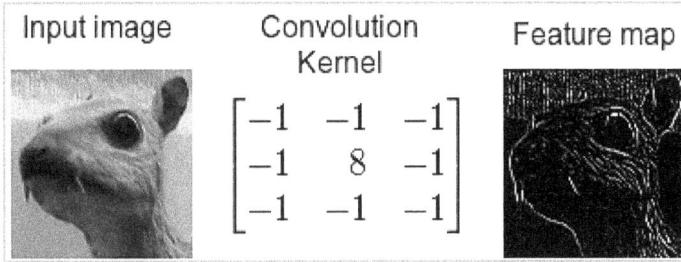

Input image

Convolution Kernel

$$\begin{bmatrix} -1 & -1 & -1 \\ -1 & 8 & -1 \\ -1 & -1 & -1 \end{bmatrix}$$

Feature map

Figure 32: '*Filter*' or '*convolution kernel*' and 'Convolved Feature' or 'Activation Map' or the '*Feature Map*'.

How Does CNN Recognize Images?

Consider the following images in **Figure 33**:

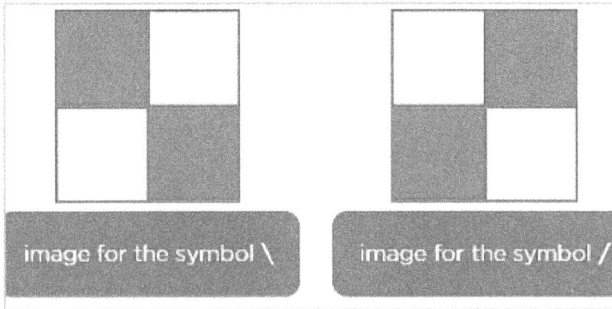

image for the symbol \   image for the symbol /

Figure 33: The boxes that are coloured represent a pixel value of 1, and 0 if not coloured.

The boxes that are coloured represent a pixel value of 1, and 0 if not coloured. When you press backslash (\), the left image of **Figure 33** gets processed. When you press forward-slash (/), the right image of **Figure 33** is processed.

Layers in a Convolutional Neural Network

A convolution neural network has multiple hidden layers that help in extracting information from an image. The four important layers in CNN are:

i. Convolution layer
ii. ReLU layer
iii. Pooling layer
iv. Fully connected layer

i.   Convolution Layer

This is the first step in the process of extracting valuable features from an image. A convolution layer has several filters that perform the convolution operation.

ii.   ReLU layer

ReLU stands for the rectified linear unit. Once the feature maps are extracted, the next step is to move them to a ReLU layer. ReLU performs an element-wise operation and sets all the negative pixels to 0. It introduces non-linearity to the network, and the generated output is a rectified feature map.

iii.   Pooling Layer

Pooling is a down-sampling operation that reduces the dimensionality of the feature map. The rectified feature map now goes through a pooling layer to generate a pooled feature map.

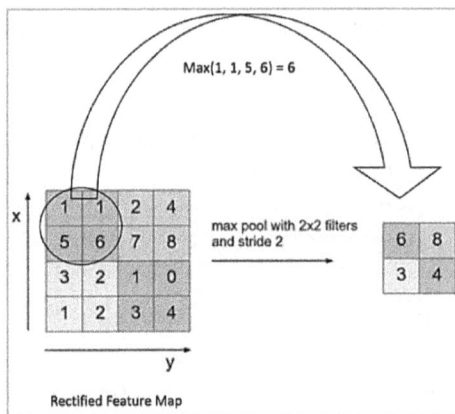

Figure 34: Max pooling.

The pooling layer uses various filters to identify distinct parts of the image like *edges, corners, body, feathers, eyes,* and *beak*. **Figure 34** shows an example of Max Pooling operation on a Rectified Feature map (obtained after convolution + ReLU operation) by using a 2×2 window. We slide our 2 x 2 window by 2 cells (also called 'stride') and take the maximum value in each region. As shown in **Figure 34**, this reduces the dimensionality of our feature map.

A convolutional neural network that can recognise characteristics like eyes, noses, faces, and legs is shown in **Figure 35**. While the second layer filters identify faces, legs, and other items that are collections of the first layer filters, the first layer filters identify eyes, noses, and other fundamental forms. This is only an illustration since convolutional filters may really identify things that are meaningless to people.

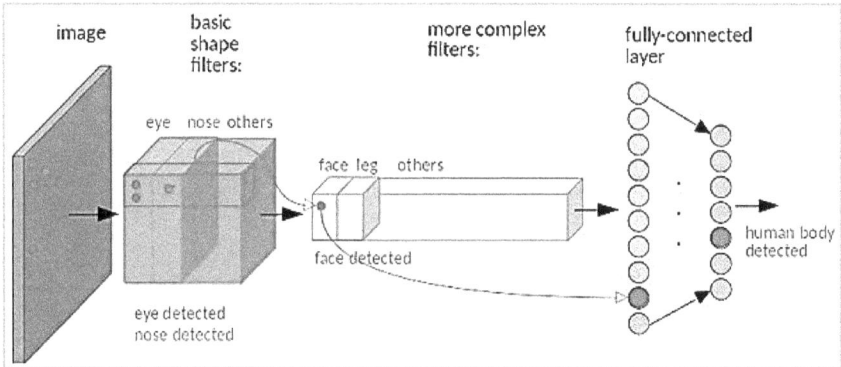

Figure 35: How a convolutional neural network able to learn features.

Convolution, ReLU and Pooling are the basic building blocks of any CNN, as shown in **Figure 36**.

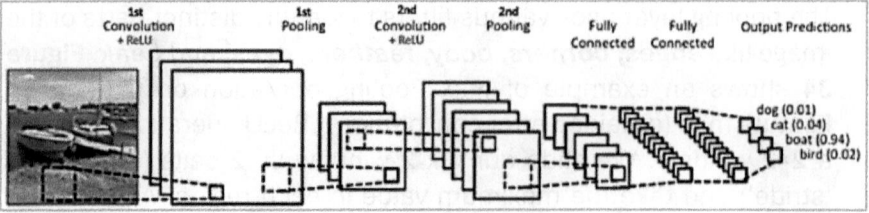

Figure 36: Basic building blocks of any CNN.

Together, these layers lower feature dimension, inject non-linearity into our network, and extract the important characteristics from the photos. The Fully Connected Layer, which we will talk about in the following section, receives its output from the Second Pooling Layer. The convolution neural network's structure, as shown in **Figure 37**, is as follows:

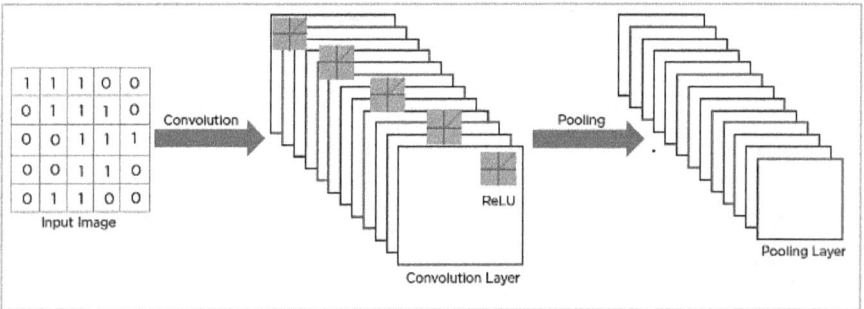

Figure 37: structure of the convolution neural network.

The next step in the process is called ***flattening***. Flattening is used to convert all the resultant 2-Dimensional arrays from ***pooled feature maps*** into a single long continuous *linear vector* as in **Figure 38**.

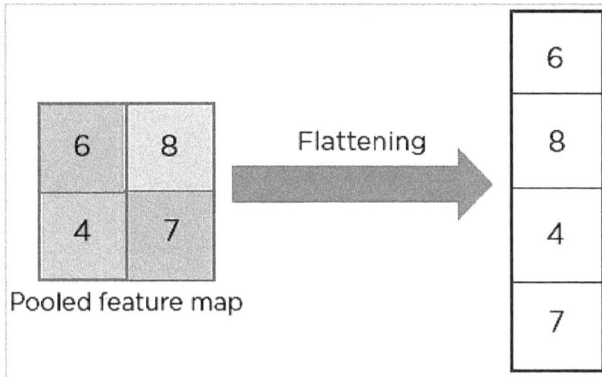

Figure 38: Process of flattening.

The flattened matrix is fed as input to the *fully connected* layer to classify the image as shown in **Figure 39**.

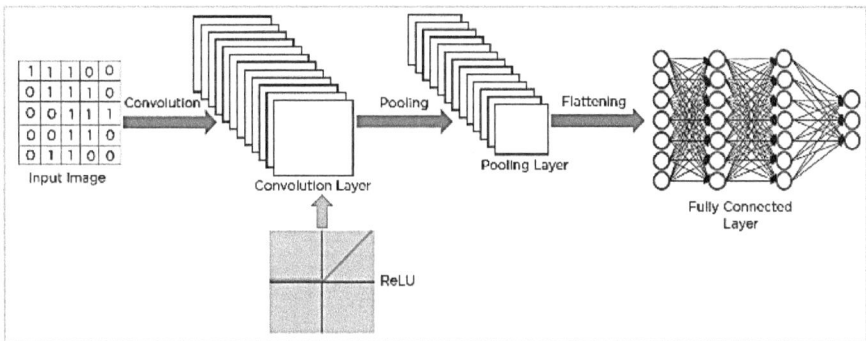

Figure 39: flattened matrix act as input to the *fully connected* layer.

iv.   Fully Connected Layer

The Fully Connected layer is a Multi-Layer Perceptron that uses a softmax activation function in the output layer. It implies that every neuron in the previous layer is connected to every neuron on the next layer as shown in **Figure 40**.

The output from the convolutional and pooling layers represents high-level features of the input image, which are used to classify the input image into various classes based on the training dataset.

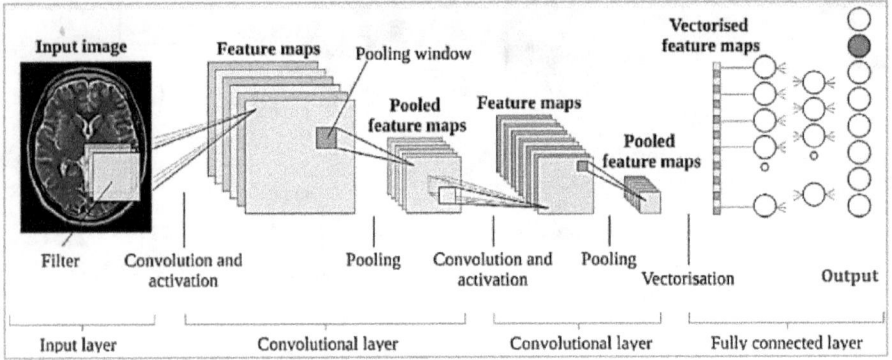

Figure 40: Building blocks of a CNN.

The sum of output probabilities from the Fully Connected Layer is 1. This is ensured by using the **Softmax** as the activation function in the output layer of the Fully Connected Layer. **Figure 41** shows how exactly CNN recognizes a bird:

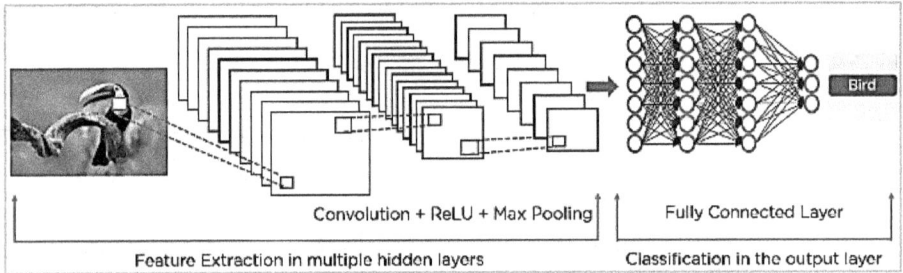

Figure 41: how exactly CNN recognizes a bird.

Definition of a NN with only one neuron after the input

```
# Definition of the network
model = Sequential()                              # starts the definition of the network
model.add(Dense(1, batch_input_shape=(None, 2),   # adds a new layer to the network with a single neuron
            activation='sigmoid'))                # The input is a tensor of size (batch_size, 2), since we don'
                                                  # chooses the activation function 'sigmoid'

# Definition of the optimizer
sgd = optimizers.SGD(lr=0.15)                     # Defining the stochastic gradient descent optimizer

# compile model
model.compile(loss='binary_crossentropy',         # compile model, which ends the definition of the model
            optimizer=sgd,
            metrics=['accuracy'])                 # using the stochastic gradient descent optimizer
```

Code Explanation:

❶ Sequential, starts the definition of the network
❷ Adds a new layer to the network with a single neuron, hence 1 in *Dense(1)*
❸ The input is a tensor of size (*Batch Size, 2*). Using **None** we don't need to specify the batch size now.
❹ Chooses the activation function **sigmoid**
❺ Defines and uses the **stochastic gradient descent** optimizer.
❻**Compiles** the model, which ends the definition of the model.

```
# summarize the architecture of the NN along with the number of weights
model.summary()

Model: "sequential"

Layer (type)                    Output Shape                Param #
=================================================================
dense (Dense)                   (None, 1)                   3
=================================================================
Total params: 3
Trainable params: 3
Non-trainable params: 0
```

We train the network by adjusting parameters using stochastic gradient descent to reduce the binary cross entropy loss function, setting the batch size to 128 every update step, and training for 400 epochs.

❼ Trains the model using the data stored in X and Y for 400 epochs
❽ Fixes the batch size to 128 examples

Let's look at the so-called learning curve, we plot the *accuracy* and *the loss vs. the epochs* as shown in **Figure 42**. You can see that after 100 epochs, we predict around 70% of our data correct and have a loss around 0.51 (these values can vary from run to run).

```
# Training of the network
history = model.fit(X, Y,        # training of the model using the training data stored in X and Y for
          epochs=400,            # for 400 epochs
          batch_size=128,        # fix the batch size to 128 examples
          verbose=0)
```

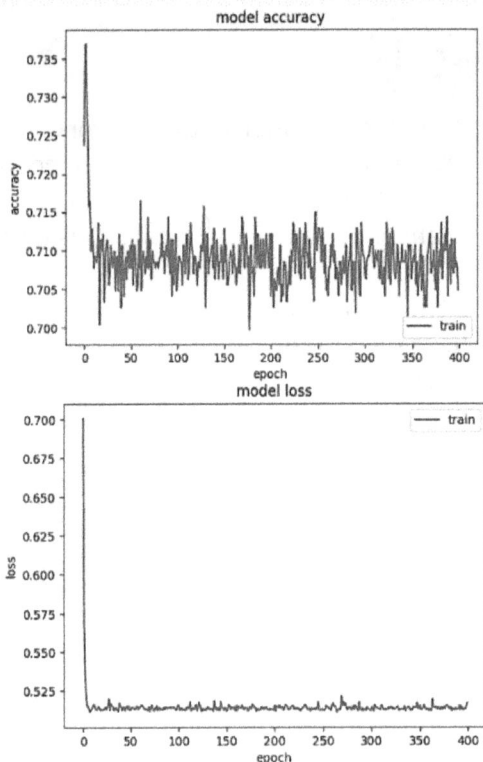

Figure 42: plot of the accuracy and the loss vs. the epochs.

Definition of the network with two hidden layers

```
# Definition of the network
model = Sequential()
model.add(Dense(8, batch_input_shape=(None, 2),activation='sigmoid'))
model.add(Dense(2, activation='softmax'))

model.compile(loss='categorical_crossentropy',
              optimizer=sgd,
              metrics=['accuracy'])
```

Code Explanation:

❶Definition of the hidden layer with *eight (8) neurons*
❷The output layer with *two (2) output* neurons

```
model.summary()
```

```
Model: "sequential_1"
```

Layer (type)	Output Shape	Param #
dense_1 (Dense)	(None, 8)	24
dense_2 (Dense)	(None, 2)	18

```
Total params: 42
Trainable params: 42
Non-trainable params: 0
```

In this output summary we see that we now have a lot more trainable parameter then before.

$$24 = inputdim \cdot outpuntdim + outputbias = 2 \cdot 8 + 8$$
$$18 = inputdim \cdot outpuntdim + outputbias = 8 \cdot 2 + 2$$

Let's look again at the learning curve, we plot the accuracy and the loss vs. the epochs as shown in **Figure 43**. You can see that after 100 epochs, we predict around 86% of our data correct and have a loss around 0.29 (these values can vary from run to run). This is better than the model without a hidden layer.

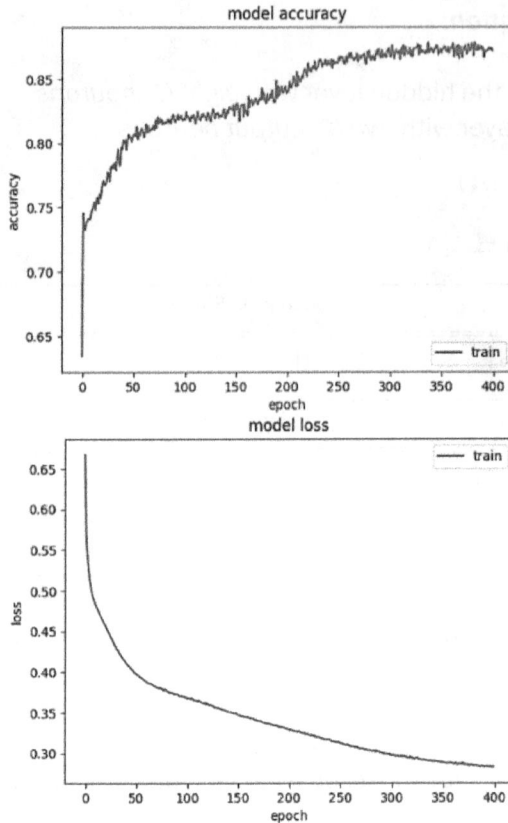

Figure 43: plot of the accuracy and the loss vs. the epochs.

What are Graph Neural Networks, and How Do They Work?

The effectiveness and simplicity of neural networks in pattern recognition and data mining have increased their popularity in recent years. Massive effort has been put into the research and development of Neural Networks as a result of Deep Learning's application to tasks like object detection and speech recognition. Graph-structured data, which is made up of a collection of nodes and the edges that describe the connections between them, is the target of Graph Neural Networks (GNNs), a particular kind of neural network. When it comes to node categorization, link prediction, and graph clustering, GNNs are immensely helpful.

In order to update the node representations, a graph neural network propagates information via a graph's edges. Up until the nodes converge to a stable representation, this procedure is done several times. Applications for graph neural networks include social network analysis, recommendation systems, drug discovery, natural language processing, and computer vision. The fundamental benefit of utilising graph neural networks is its propensity to handle complicated graph-structured data, capture non-linear interactions between nodes, and generalise to new data. GNNs are a flexible tool for several applications since they can be utilised for both supervised and unsupervised learning tasks.

Due to its random, complex topology, and unfixed node ordering, CNN on graph data is computationally difficult to accomplish. When the graph structure is noisy or lacking, GNNs can over fit and become computationally costly, especially for big networks. Utilising CNN on graph data becomes challenging as a result.

Classification of Neural Network Hyper-parameters

Hyper-parameters control the behaviour and structure of the neural network models. So, it is really important to learn more about what each hyper-parameter does [2, 4, 7].

- In ML and DL algorithms, parameters and hyper parameters are variables, but there are distinctions between them.
- The training process involves updating parameters, which are variables that are learnt from the data.
- Before the model is trained, hyper parameters are settings made by the ML engineer or another individual.
- To create better models, they must be actively changed because they are not automatically taught from the data.
- In machine learning and deep learning, determining the best values for hyper parameters can be difficult since they vary depending on the size, complexity, and nature of the dataset and the issue at hand.

Neural network hyper-parameters can be classified as follows:

Classification of Neural Network
Hyperparameters

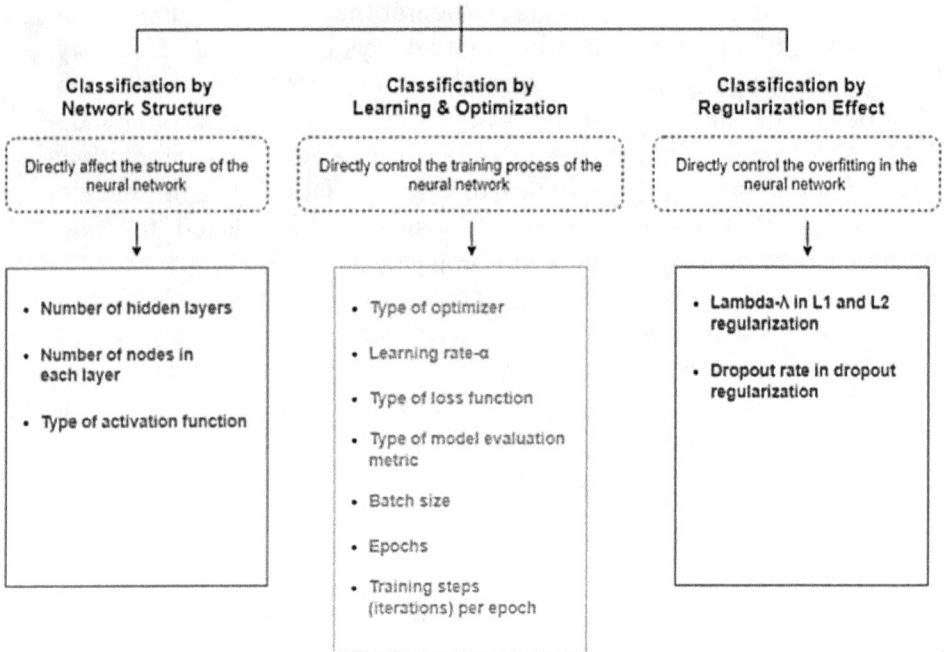

Classification by Network Structure	Classification by Learning & Optimization	Classification by Regularization Effect
Directly affect the structure of the neural network	Directly control the training process of the neural network	Directly control the overfitting in the neural network
• Number of hidden layers • Number of nodes in each layer • Type of activation function	• Type of optimizer • Learning rate-α • Type of loss function • Type of model evaluation metric • Batch size • Epochs • Training steps (iterations) per epoch	• Lambda-Λ in L1 and L2 regularization • Dropout rate in dropout regularization

- ***Number of hidden layers***

This is also called the depth of the network. The term "deep" in deep learning refers to the number of hidden layers (depth) of a neural network.

- ***Number of nodes (neurons/units) in each layer***

The network's ability to learn is influenced by how many hidden units are present in each hidden layer. While too few hidden units produce smaller networks that may *underfit* the training data, too many hidden units result in huge networks that may *overfit* the data.

- ***Type of activation function***

The activation function utilised in the layers is the last hyper-parameter that describes the network topology. While the hidden layers must utilise an activation function to introduce non-linearity, the input layer does not. The kind of problem being solved dictates the kind of activation that is utilised in the output layer.

- Regression: Identity activation function with one node
- Binary classification: Sigmoid activation function with one node
- Multiclass classification: Softmax activation function with one node per class
- Multi label classification: Sigmoid activation function with one node per class

- ***Type of optimizer***

By altering network settings, the optimizer algorithm reduces the loss function. One of the most well-known algorithms has three variations: gradient descent.

- Batch gradient descent
- Stochastic gradient descent
- Mini-batch gradient descent

All these variants differ in the **batch size** that we use to compute the gradient of the loss function.

Other types of optimizers that have been developed to deal with the shortcomings of the gradient descent algorithm are:

- Gradient descent with momentum
- Adam
- Adagrad
- Adadelta
- Adamax
- Nadam
- Ftrl
- RMSProp (Keras default)

- ***Learning rate-α***

In training neural networks, the learning rate is a crucial hyper parameter. It controls the rate at which the optimizer descends the error curve, and the gradient (derivative) controls the step's direction. If the network takes too long to converge, it is preferable to start with a low learning rate, such as 0.001, and subsequently raise it.

- *Type of loss function*

Utilising an optimizer, such as Mean Squared Error (MSE) or Mean Absolute Error (MAE), to reduce the loss function is the objective of training a neural network. Utilising an optimizer, such as Mean Squared Error (MSE) or Mean Absolute Error (MAE), allows for this.

- *Type of model evaluation metric*

A neural network's performance during testing is gauged using evaluation metrics. **Accuracy, precision, recall, and AUC** metrics are utilised for classification jobs whereas mean squared error and mean absolute error are employed for regression tasks.

- *Batch size*

The **model.fit()** function includes the batch size as a key hyper parameter. It is referring to how many training instances are in the batch. 16, 32, 64, 128, 256, 512, 1024 are typical values. While a lower batch size converges more quickly over fewer epochs, a bigger batch size demands more processing resources per epoch.

- *Epochs*

The epochs is another important hyper parameter that is found in the **model.fit()** method. Epochs refer to the number of times the model sees the entire dataset. The number of **epochs** should be increased when,

- The network is trained with a small learning rate.
- The batch size is too small.

Sometimes, the network will tend to $overfit$ the training data with a large number of epochs. That is, after converging, the validation error begins to increase at some point while the training error is further decreasing. When that happens, the model performs well on the training data and but poorly generalizes on new unseen data. At that point, we should stop the training process. This is called *early stopping* as shown in **Figure 44**.

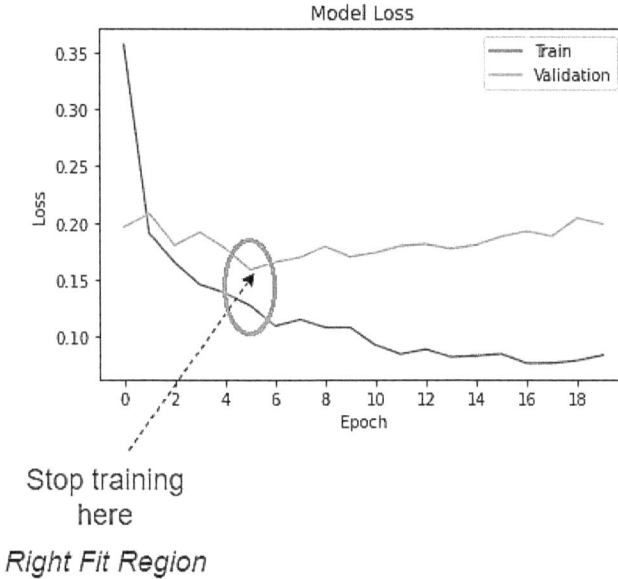

Figure 44: Early stopping process.

Neural Network: Industry Use Cases

Artificial neural networks (ANNs) may categorise information, cluster data, or forecast outcomes since they are trained on historical data. A variety of activities may be performed with ANNs, including data analysis, audio to text transcription, facial recognition software, and weather forecasting.

- For difficult non-linear problems, such fraud detection, business lapse/churn analysis, risk analysis, and data mining, neural networks can offer extremely precise and reliable solutions [20].
- Their key advantage is the automated inference of the task-performer's approach from the data.
- Furthermore, compared to traditional rule-based systems and fuzzy systems, they operate far more efficiently and use significantly less storage.
- They also include a natural type of regularisation or generalisation, which makes them very resistant to erratic, inaccurate, or lacking data.

Top Companies using Artificial Neural Network (ANN):

- Nvidia Corp. (NVDA)
- Alphabet (GOOG, GOOGL)
- Salesforce.com (CRM)
- Amazon.com (AMZN)
- Microsoft Corp. (MSFT)
- Twilio (TWLO)
- IBM (IBM)
- Facebook (FB)

Conclusion

Because they don't need explicit programming and can handle loud, inaccurate, or missing data, neural computers are perfect for commercial and military applications.

Industrial Applications using Neural Networks

Artificial neural networks are now a common information processing method, which has given rise to a number of businesses uses for both goods and services [11, 12]. Both the civic and military sectors have enormous potential.

Given below are domains of commercial applications of neural network technology:

- **Business** - Marketing, Real Estate
- **Document & Form Processing** - Machine printed character recognition, Graphics recognition, Hand printed character recognition, Cursive handwritten character recognition.
- **Finance Industry** - Market trading, Fraud detection, Credit rating.
- **Food industry** - Odour/aroma analysis, Product development, Quality assurance
- **Energy Industry** - Electrical load forecasting, hydroelectric dam operation, Natural gas
- **Manufacturing Process control** - Quality control

- **Medical & Health Care Industry** - Image analysis Drug development, Resource allocation [8].
- **Science & Engineering** - Chemical engineering, Electrical engineering, Weather forecasting
- **Transportation & Communication**

Some applications of neural networks are:

o Forecasting the Behaviour of Complex Systems
o Signal Processing
o Data Compression
o Paint Quality Inspection
o DNA Sequence Analysis

MLPs have been successful at a wide range of AI tasks, from speech recognition [13] to predicting thermal conductivity of aqueous electrolyte solutions [14] and controlling a continuous stirred-tank reactor [15]. For example, an MLP for recognizing printed digits (e.g., the account and routing number printed on a check) would be comprised of a grid of inputs to read individual pixels of digits (say, a 9×12 bitmap), followed by one or more hidden layers, and finally 10 output neurons to indicate which number was recognized in the input (0–9) (**Figure 45**).

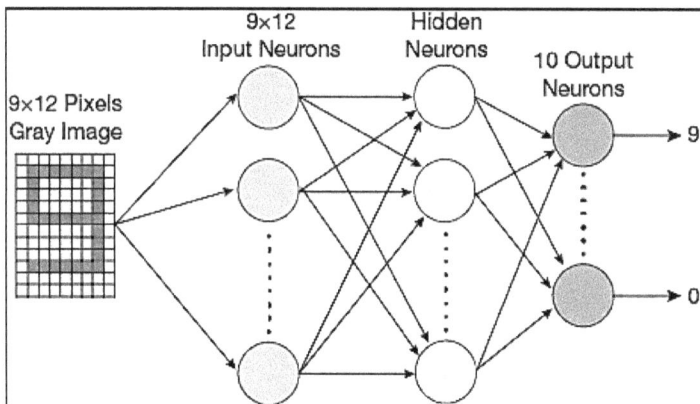

Figure 45: A multilayer perceptron for reading cheque numbers would comprise a grid of inputs, hidden neurons, and 10 output neurons to show which number was recognised.

Researchers trained an MLP to predict a compound's viscosity using data from Perry's Chemical Engineers' Handbook [16]. By teaching an MLP to recognise variations in temperature and flow rate, researchers in another study were able to identify defects in a heat exchanger [17].

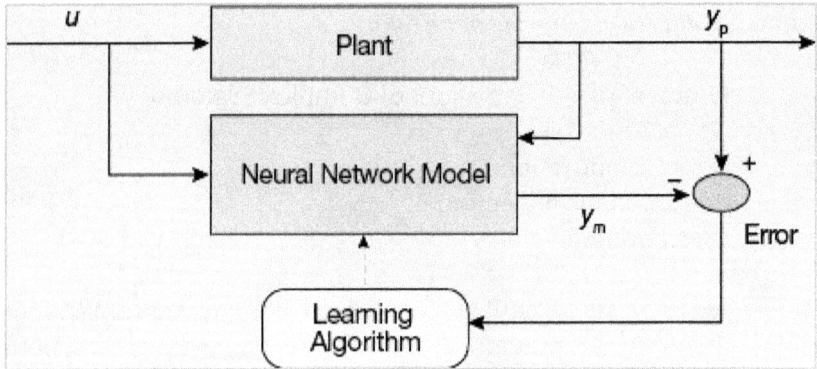

Figure 46: By analysing the discrepancy between a plants' real output and the output of its neural network, an MLP can discover the dynamics of the system.

As another example, MLPs have been used for predictive control of chemical reactors [18]. The typical setup trains a neural network to learn the forward dynamics of the plant. The prediction error between the plant output and the neural network output is used for training the neural network (**Figure 46**).

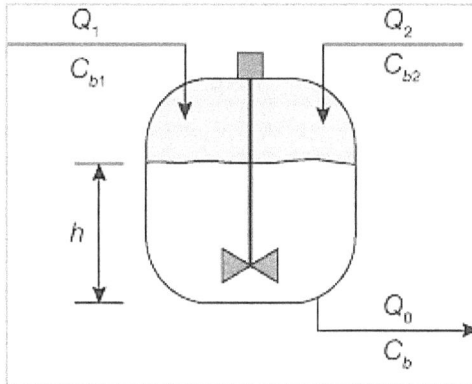

Figure 47: A continuous stirred-tank reactor can be trained to maintain appropriate product concentration and flow by using past data.

The neural network learns from previous inputs and outputs to predict future values of the plant output. For example, a controller for a catalytic continuous stirred-tank reactor (as in **Figure 47**) can be trained to maintain appropriate product concentration and flow by using past data about inflow Q_1 and Q_2 at concentrations C_{b1} and C_{b2}, respectively, liquid level h, and outflow Q_0 at concentration C_b.

Real-Life and Business Applications of Neural Networks

*Here's a list of other neural network engineering **Real-Life** applications currently in use in various industries:*

- **Aerospace:** Simulations of aircraft components, control systems, auto-piloting, and flight paths.
- **Automotive:** The following improvements are required: better power trains, virtual sensors, guiding systems, and warranty activity analysers.
- **Electronics:** Skills in speech synthesis, machine vision, non-linear modelling, code sequence prediction, process management, and chip failure analysis are all crucial.
- **Manufacturing:** Chemical product design analysis, dynamic modelling of chemical process systems, process control, process and machine diagnosis, product design and

analysis, paper quality forecasting, project bidding, planning, and management, quality analysis of computer chips, visual quality inspection systems, and welding quality analysis.

- **Mechanics:** Condition monitoring, systems modelling, and control
- **Robotics:** Forklift robots, manipulator controllers, trajectory control, and vision systems
- **Telecommunications:** Network design, administration, routing, and control, ATM network control, automated information services, customer payment processing systems, data compression, equalisers, fault management, handwriting recognition, real-time spoken language translation, and pattern recognition.

Here are further current examples of Neural Networks ***business applications:***

- **Banking:** Loan delinquencies, fraud and risk assessment, credit and loan application review, and credit card attrition are all crucial.
- **Business Analytics:** Market research, market mix, market structure, customer behaviour modelling, customer segmentation, fraud propensity, and models for attrition, default, buy, and renewals are crucial.
- **Defence:** Object discrimination, sensors, sonar, radar, image signal processing, signal/image identification, target tracking, and weapon steering are used in counterterrorism.
- **Education:** Software for adaptive learning, dynamic forecasting, study of the educational system, modelling of student performance [20], and personality profiling.
- **Financial:** Ratings of corporate bonds, financial analysis, analysis of how credit lines are used, forecasting the value of currencies, loan counselling, mortgage screening, appraisal, and portfolio trading.
- **Medical:** Cancer cell analysis, ECG and EEG analysis, test recommendations for ERs, cost-saving measures, transplant procedure optimisation, and prosthetic design [8, 19].

- **Securities:** Automatic bond rating, market analysis, and stock trading advisory systems
- **Transportation:** Routing systems, truck brake diagnosis systems, and vehicle scheduling

The way individuals do business is being transformed by neural networks.

Conclusions

The many neural network types, their activation mechanisms, when to utilise them, their graphs, and code snippets are the most crucial information in this literature. These facts provide an overview of the many forms of neural networks and will assist you in becoming more familiar with the idea of neural networks.

A neural network is formed of neurons connected by synapses, which simulate the rate at which the neurons fire. The basic unit of a neural network is a perceptron, and multilayer perceptrons can be utilised when a single perceptron fails owing to the dataset's nonlinearity.

Future of Neural Networks

*Here are some likely **future developments** in neural network technologies:*

Fuzzy Logic Integration: Fuzzy logic recognises notions that are relative as well as true and false values. Applications include auto-engineering, building crane control, glaucoma monitoring, and candidate screening for jobs. Future neural network applications will require fuzzy logic as a fundamental component.

Pulsed Neural Networks: Mammalian biological brain networks employ pulsing to transport information and carry out calculations, according to findings from neurobiological experiments. The advancement of theoretical analysis, model-building, neurobiological modelling, and hardware deployment to make computing more like human brains has been driven by this realisation.

Specialized Hardware: Deep learning, machine learning, and neural networks are undergoing rapid hardware development due to the rapid development of neural network processing units (NNPUs) and other AI-specific hardware, commonly referred to as neuro-synaptic architectures. Neuro-synaptic chips are essential to the development of AI, as they operate more like a biological brain than a standard computer's core.

Improvement of Existing Technologies: Modern neural network technologies, new software and hardware, and the enhanced computational capacity of neuro-synaptic designs have all made neural networks possible.

Robotics: Robots have been prophesied to be able to feel, observe, and anticipate the environment around them. Yonck, a futurist, believes that there is still a long way to go before robots can think in a flexible, non-brittle fashion. He believes that although these robots are learning in a restricted fashion, it would be a huge jump to suggest that they are "thinking".

References

[1] Zhou, Zhi-Hua. Machine learning. Springer Nature, 2021.

[2] Heaton, Jeff. "Ian Goodfellow, Yoshua Bengio, and Aaron Courville: Deep learning: The MIT Press, 2016, 800 pp, ISBN: 0262035618." Genetic Programming and Evolvable Machines 19, no. 1-2 (2018): 305-307.

[3] Roberts, Daniel A., Sho Yaida, and Boris Hanin. The principles of deep learning theory. Cambridge, MA, USA: Cambridge University Press, 2022.

[4] Bishop, Christopher M., and Nasser M. Nasra badi. Pattern recognition and machine learning. Vol. 4, no. 4. New York: springer, 2006.

[5] Aggarwal, Charu C., and Charu C. Aggarwal. "Machine learning with shallow neural networks." Neural Networks and Deep Learning: A Textbook (2018): 53-104.

[6] Aggarwal, Charu C. "Neural networks and deep learning." Springer 10, no. 978 (2018): 3.

[7] Nielsen, Michael A. Neural networks and deep learning. Vol. 25. San Francisco, CA, USA: Determination press, 2015.

[8] Ghosh, Partha. "Deep Learning to Diagnose Diseases and Security in 5G Healthcare Informatics." In Machine Learning and Deep Learning Techniques for Medical Science, pp. 279-331. CRC Press, 2022.

[9] Moawad, Ahmed W., David T. Fuentes, Mohamed G. El Banan, Ahmed S. Shalaby, Jeffrey Guccione, Serageldin Kamel, Corey T. Jensen, and Khaled M. Elsayes. "Artificial intelligence in diagnostic radiology: Where do we stand, challenges, and opportunities." Journal of computer assisted tomography 46, no. 1 (2022): 78-90.

[10] Kizilkan, Zeynep Burcu, Mahmut Sami Sivri, Ibrahim Yazici, and Omer Faruk Beyca. "Neural Networks and Deep Learning." In Business Analytics for Professionals, pp. 127-151. Cham: Springer International Publishing, 2022.

[11] Kandi, Haribabu, Deepak Mishra, and Subrahmanyam RK Sai Gorthi. "Exploring the learning capabilities of convolutional neural networks for robust image watermarking." Computers & Security 65 (2017): 247-268.

[12] Soni, Mukesh, S. Gomathi, Pankaj Kumar, Prathamesh P. Churi, Mazin Abed Mohammed, and Akbal Omran Salman. "Hybridizing

convolutional neural network for classification of lung diseases." International Journal of Swarm Intelligence Research (IJSIR) 13, no. 2 (2022): 1-15.

[13] Azzizi, Norelhouda, Abdelouhab Zaatri, and A. L. G. E. R. I. A. Constantine. "A Learning Process Of Multilayer Perceptron for Speech Recognition." International Journal of Pure and Applied Mathematics 107, no. 4 (2016): 1005-1012.

[14] Eslamloueyan, Reza, Mohammad H. Khademi, and Saeed Mazinani. "Using a multilayer perceptron network for thermal conductivity prediction of aqueous electrolyte solutions." Industrial & engineering chemistry research 50, no. 7 (2011): 4050-4056.

[15] Eslamloueyan, Reza, Mohammad H. Khademi, and Saeed Mazinani. "Using a multilayer perceptron network for thermal conductivity prediction of aqueous electrolyte solutions." Industrial & engineering chemistry research 50, no. 7 (2011): 4050-4056.

[16] Moghadassi, Abdolreza, Fahime Parvizian, and Sayed Mohsen Hosseini. "Application of Artificial Neural Network for Prediction of Liquid Viscosity." Indian Chemical Engineer 52, no. 1 (2010): 37-48.

[17] Himmelblau, D. M., R. W. Barker, and W. Suewatanakul. "Fault classification with the aid of artificial neural networks." In Fault Detection, Supervision and Safety for Technical Processes 1991, pp. 541-545. Pergamon, 1992.

[18] Vasičkaninová, Anna, and Monika Bakošová. "Neural network predictive control of a chemical reactor." Acta Chimica Slovaca 2, no. 2 (2009): 21-36.

[19] P. Ghosh. "Timely Diabetes Possibility Prediction using AI Techniques", Journal of Artificial Intelligence Research & Advances, 9(2) (2022).

[20] Ghosh, Partha. "Data mining approach to predict academic performance of students." BOHR International Journal of Computer Science 2, no. 1 (2023): 21-31.

[21] Ghosh, P., and S. Ghosh. "IoT and machine learning in green smart home automation and green building management." J Altern Energy Sourc Technol 10, no. 3 (2020): 8-36.